Hines Sight

Hines Sight

Frazer Hines

First published in a different form as *Films, Farms and Fillies* by Boxtree Ltd in 1997

Editor: Sam Stone
Production Manager: David J Howe
Design and Layout: Arnold T Blumberg

ISBN: 978-1-84583-998-7

Hines Sight © 1996, 2009 Frazer Hines

The moral right of the author has been asserted.

Printed in Great Britain by the MPG Books Group, Bodmin and King's Lynn

1 2 3 4 5 6 7 8 9 10 11 12 13 14 15

British Library Cataloguing in Publication Data.
A catalogue record for this book is available from the British Library.

Dedication

I would like to dedicate this book to:

Shaun Sutton, without whom my television career would not have started; and another lady in my life who has never answered back, given me much fun racing and borne me numerous children who are galloping about the race courses of England: Excavator Lady.

Acknowledgements

Thanks to Sam and David for helping me to get this book going and to all my friends who are no longer with me but who have given me much love and affection throughout my lifetime.

Thanks to you all.

Foreword

Our friendship with Frazer has lasted longer than most show-business marriages! 35 years.

Our first meeting was in Jersey where we were appearing in summer season. Frazer was visiting Jersey for a few days holiday with *Emmerdale Farm* scripts in hand.

We were told that Joe Sugden was in the audience and Ian was quick to inform us all that the actor also played Jamie in *Doctor Who*. So we were looking forward to meeting him after the show.

We hit it off so well that for the rest of Frazer's holiday our friendship developed, with days on the beach swimming in the sea and partying at night after the show … oh to be young. I don't think that Frazer learned much of his scripts over those four days and nights.

On his return to Yorkshire, he sent us a telegram reading: 'Brilliant Young Actor Returns Home Safely From Third Rate Cabaret Act's Hideaway In Jersey'. Three years later, in 1978, he sent us another telegram, this time to The London Palladium where we were appearing in our first Royal Variety Show. The message read: 'Brilliant Young Actor Now Recognises Third Rate Cabaret Act As Top Of The Bill'. This was typical of Frazer – a great sense of humour which he has sustained for all these years.

Our friendship continued to grow and we went to all his weddings and enjoyed sailing in Guernsey when he would come over to play cricket for The Lord's Taverners, a charity which he does endless work for.

Two years ago Frazer came to stay with us in our apartment on the Gold Coast in Australia. What a great time we had. It was as though the years had never passed. We played golf, went cycling, and enjoyed clubbing at night. Only this time it was the Bowls Club not the night clubs … we all have our bus passes now!

Frazer is never anything but enthusiastic, and this spills over into the pages of this book. We're sure you will take away the sheer passion Frazer has for life and show-business, and of course not forgetting his great love of horses both as owner and jockey.

Frazer became a fellow Brother Water Rat a couple of years ago, this says much about how highly Frazer is considered among his fellow actors and performers, as to become a member of The Grand Order Of Water Rats is one of the greatest accolades that show-business can bestow.

We are pleased and proud to be asked to pen this little piece for the new edition of his autobiography, and we hope that Frazer's warmth and humour rubs off on you, as it did on us all those years ago.

Ian and Janette Krankie
November 2009

Chapter One
Childhood Days

'**W**elcome to Bath Races,' announced the tannoy. 'The first race today will be two o'clock selling …'

As the tannoy faded into the distance, a little boy tugged at his mother's skirt.

'Mummy, will you put me sixpence each way on this horse called Wildcat?'

'All right Frazer. I'll do that for you.'

Yes, that was me. At Bath Races. Aged twelve. My first punt and Wildcat won at six-to-one. That started my spiral up into horse ownership and horse breeding, one of the passions of my life. There have been others, of course, but that's where my love affair with horses started. Women – we'll come to them in due course. And the acting? That came much earlier. But before even that, just like the horse, I have to get started.

I was born in a little place just outside Leeds called Horsforth. Don't feel bad if you've never heard of it. Almost nobody has.

I was the third son of Molly and Bill Hines, although I wasn't meant to be a boy. With two lads already, Roy and Iain, Mum and Dad just sort of assumed they were due for a girl. So they laid in a complete set of pink blankets and nightdresses, and decked a cot in frills and pretty pink ribbons. A little daughter, they thought, would just complete the family nicely. They had quite decided to call me Heather. That plan went the way of all flesh when I turned up, a strapping baby boy.

We moved to Harrogate soon afterwards. While my father went out to work every day, my mother ran a boarding house at 18 St Mary's Avenue. If people ever ask me, I always say that I was born in Harrogate. It was a wonderful place to grow up, my mother's boarding house. There were always such interesting people around. There were sales reps staying, and also famous entertainers – band leaders like Cyril Stapleton and Nat Gonnella. The boarding house was exactly right for mother; she was an outgoing woman who loved a house full of people.

My mother served the food with the help of two Newcastle girls, Eunice and Gloria. Roy and I helped serve the teas in the afternoon, and often we would see this huge pile of beautiful cakes being taken through to the dining-room. Boy, would our mouths water! Of course, all the best cakes were always taken by the customers, the meringues, the éclairs and so on, leaving the stodgy, boring ones uneaten. I remember Roy saying to me one day in front of the guests, 'Next time, Frazer, we'll choose our cakes before the guests get theirs.' Needless to say, Mum squashed that idea flat. We didn't even get the leftovers that day.

Growing up in Harrogate was great fun. We used to play on The Stray, a huge expanse of green, green grass. It's still there. It covers miles and miles of Harrogate, and for a townie boy it was every exciting landscape he could conjure. It was the prairies of the Wild West, Berlin during the War, it was the Somme; deathless adventures were had there, countless battles fought, from the Little Big Horn to the Battle of the Bulge to knights rescuing damsels – you name it, it was there.

We were a happy family, and, as is often the case with northern families, my mother was the driving force. She was a fierce Scot with enormous energy, always ready to fight her corner. My father was a quiet man who hated rows and sharp words. If Roy and Iain and I had been naughty, mum would say, 'Speak to them Bill,' and he would sigh and reluctantly perform his fatherly duty.

'Hello, boys,' he would say, and this friendly overture would be enough to drive her crazy.

Most summer holidays were spent either careering down Cold Bath Road in wheeled soap boxes, or driving with my mother, father and brothers up to Scotland to stay with my grandmother. She had a big old house overlooking the River Clyde at Port Glasgow and we spent most of our summer holidays there. I went back to have a look at it many years later, but the house was no longer there. It had been torn down and a block of flats now occupies the site where it stood. Such is progress.

In those heady summer days when the Majorcas, Ibizas and Greek islands were nothing more than travel agents' El Dorados, when most people in England holidayed in Britain, we would go, as they say in Scotland, 'doon the watter', travelling from Largs to Cairn, Dunoon, Innellan and Rothesay. I can still hear the boatman cry the place-names as we waited for the steamer. The *Saint Columba* or perhaps two old paddle steamers: the *Waverley* – still sailing now off Bournemouth Pier – and of course the old *Jeanie Deans*.

Years later I saw the *Waverley* again when I was playing in *Doctor in the House* down at Bournemouth Theatre. One day I even went out for a trip in her. As she sailed off the Dorset coast on that sunny day, I looked out over the sea and suddenly I was transported back in time. I was that little boy in a kilt again, clutching an ice-cream in one hand while holding my grandmother's hand with the other.

We had two uncles living in Scotland – Mum's brothers: Uncle Roy and Uncle Jack – and they used to play in the band on the *Saint Columba*. We used to go and see them working as we went 'doon the watter' round the Kyles of Bute and back home. But when I saw Uncle Roy and Uncle Jack playing on the ship, I nearly caused a disaster at sea, because, with reckless impulse I shouted out, 'Oh Look! A band on ship!'

The cry was taken up: abandon ship! Everyone rushed for their lifejackets.

No, not really! Those who know me realise quite quickly that I have something of a mind for jokes, puns and quips. They escape from me all the time, and sometimes it's hard to control myself. So this book is no exception … watch out for them!

Uncle Roy and Uncle Jack also played at a theatre near Largs called Cragburn and many's the time we would go and see them perform in the summer shows there. Uncle Roy eventually married one of the showgirls – my Auntie Mary. He always had an eye for the girls. I've often wondered if I inherited this from him.

On Sundays we might get into our grandmother's old Armstrong Siddeley car and drive off to the Buchanan Arms in our best kilts for a roast lunch. The Buchanan is still there to this day and I occasionally revisit it for old time's sake.

Those were great days – when one was young and innocent up in the isles of Scotland. My Uncle Tommy Dans, mother's cousin, used to take Roy and I out fishing and peat-cutting on the Isle of Harris. Roy and I used to make little wooden boats with lead weights in the bottom and linoleum sails. Then we would sail them up and down the lochs. Or we explored an old shipwreck just off the bay by Stornoway with our uncles. My Scottish heritage and those idyllic holidays with my grandmother stood me in very good stead later in my life when I spent several happy years pretending to be Scottish as Jamie in *Doctor Who*. I even got to wear a kilt again!

We were great picture-goers. Iain would take Roy and I to see Dick Foran and

Peggy Moran in *The Mummy's Hand* or some other horror film, and then he'd chase us home, screaming and capering like the hunchback of Notre Dame, or walking like a zombie with dead eyes and arms outstretched. Like little boys everywhere we thrilled to the delicious terror, scaring ourselves silly. We saw one film called *The Wolf Man*; Iain had this wolf mask that he put on to chase us all the way home.

We hared around the corners shrieking 'The wolf man's after us!'

There was in one street a frail old man leaning heavily on a walking stick, who stopped us and said, 'Wolf man, you say?'

'Yes, he's after us!'

The man shook his head over the hyperactive imaginations of small boys. We ran past him and Iain immediately came growling round the corner in his mask. The old boy took one look at Iain, dropped his walking stick and legged it like an Olympic sprinter. We never knew what happened to that man; he could still be running for all we know.

The music for those old films always seemed to be conducted or arranged by a chap called Muir Mathieson. I was to meet the grand man many years later when I got a small part in the 1963 film *I Could Go On Singing* which starred Judy Garland and Dirk Bogarde. When I was a young boy at Harrogate I attended Norwood College and this was what helped me get the part. Norwood College was a boys-only school, but we did a lot of Gilbert and Sullivan productions there and among other things, I played Little Buttercup in *HMS Pinafore*. When we all auditioned years later at Corona (my acting school) for *I Could Go On Singing*, young Hines piped up, 'I can sing Gilbert and Sullivan, sir,' which I did. And as a result I got one of the parts in the film with Judy Garland, although it is one of my regrets that I never actually got to meet that great star. The scene I was in was where she visited her son's school performing *HMS Pinafore*. We had to dress as girls or boys and luckily I drew the long straw and got to dress as a boy this time!

With the earnings from my mother's boarding house we were the first in our street to have television. Across the road from us there was a very poor family, the Trelfalls. I knew Norman Trelfall, son of the house, because we used to attend Western Board Primary School together before I went to Norwood College. The Trelfalls used to go and stand or sit outside the local television shop in Harrogate and watch the flickering grey images of the TV screen in the window. Just pictures – they couldn't hear the sound through the glass. We passed them one night, the whole family sitting on wooden boxes watching the television. Norman was lying on two planks of wood resting on orange boxes, with an army blanket and an old striped pillow.

'What's the matter with Norman?' I asked.

'He's got the 'flu, but he didn't want to miss this programme.'

On Coronation Day in 1953 my mother came very proudly into our bedrooms and said, 'It's the coronation of your Queen today. We're going to have a running buffet.'

We invited all the neighbours round to watch our television set. There was no 46-inch screen and surround sound systems back then. The screen was about six inches by six inches and black and white of course – but had a magnifying glass, a great innovation in its time. It magnified the picture so that the whole room of people, my family and all our neighbours, could watch the Queen being crowned.

These days every child of ten has a television set in their bedroom. It seems incredible that in the course of my short life we have come so far. In more recent years, I was attending one of my favourite pastimes, a celebrity cricket match. During the tea interval I found myself sitting with the author Jilly Cooper and enjoying a glass of chilled white wine. Jilly had bowled the first ball of the match and we were hot and sticky and giggling like children. We chatted about our childhoods – playing outside on heady summer days and coming in dirty and tired for our tea. We ended up only slightly drunk and feeling, in a funny way, a little sorry for today's children. Suppose they come to write their life stories – what can they write about? 'The day I sat in front of my television with my Nintendo', or 'The day I surfed the internet.' They've lost so much of their childhood with this modern technology. They don't seem to build racing cars out of wooden soapboxes any more. They don't seem to have an old orange box and a bald tennis ball to play tennis with. Today's child might have the virtual reality of technological wizardry, but I had the virtual reality of The Stray, which was limitless, confined only by where my imagination could take me. Progress certainly has a lot to answer for.

You'll have gathered that mother was something of an extrovert and she was also a performer. My mother and father were in the Operatic Society in Harrogate. I'm very proud of the association because I was President of the Harrogate Operatic Society for ten years. They did many shows. My mother would take named parts like Mamie Clancy in *The Belle of New York*, Clotilde Lombaste in *The New Moon*, Yum Yum in *The Mikado,* and my father was content to be in the chorus.

One time, though, he was given some lines to speak. Mum was on the stage when his moment arrived. I was sitting in the audience with Eunice, who was my mother's helper in the Bed and Breakfast, and she was looking after me that night. As my dad went to speak, I stood up and said in a loud voice, 'Daddy, I've got ice-cream.'

After all that time in the chorus, and finally with words of his own to speak, my father was struck dumb.

Roy was just as bad. In one of the shows my mum's character was assaulted. Roy jumped up and shouted, 'Nasty man, leave my mother alone!'

I attended the Margery Newbury School of Dancing on Saturday mornings, and I was generally acknowledged to have an aptitude for dance. At any rate, I clearly enjoyed performing. I never minded missing the odd Saturday with my pals, in order to go singing at a hospital or whatever was on. I was singing and playing the banjo, and dancing in various shows.

Every year Margery staged what she called 'A Fantasy'. During the fifth Fantasy I found myself singing the song 'Louise', the old Maurice Chevalier number. Now, I cannot stand itchy clothing next to my skin. I have always hated it. I could never have joined the army and worn those horrible serge trousers. I hate the feel of it moving against me and I can't move in it. For my impersonation of Maurice Chevalier my mother had bought some old potato sacking, dyed it, and made me a white suit. The minute I put the suit on I knew I wouldn't be able to wear it. I tried to move in it, but it made me walk very awkwardly.

'Mum I can't wear these trousers.'

'Don't be silly,' said my mother, 'You'll be alright.'

So I had to go on stage to sing the song.

'Every leedle breeze sims to wheesper Loueeze ...'

I was wearing a white jacket, white trousers, holding a little cane and a straw boater. When it came to the tap number in the middle-eight of the song I could not bear to bend my legs. I tap-danced with my knees rigid like a cross between Fred Astaire and Douglas Bader.

The next day the papers reported, 'Seven year old stops the show. Not only could he sing with the French voice of Maurice Chevalier, he even had the stiff-legged walk of the old troubadour. A young star is born here tonight at the Royal Hall Harrogate.' Word travelled fast and a lady came up from London to see me and said I ought to audition for the Corona Academy of Stage Training – at the time one of the leading acting schools, along with Aida Foster and Italia Conti. Which I did. Rona Knight, the founder and head of the Academy, passed me with flying colours, and I joined Corona. This may have been the best thing that ever happened to me.

Girls and the opposite sex have featured heavily in my life, as you'll come to realise. The first girl that caught my eye lived at the top of my street, and her parents ran a sweet shop. Diane used to give me Mars bars in exchange for the odd kiss. I'll never forget Diane … But nothing compares with my first day at Corona Academy. My mother took me into the playground. I was met by the school captain. A tall, beautiful, long-legged blonde in school uniform, by the name of Carol Olver. I looked around. There was another girl there, later to become a girlfriend, Vicky Harrington. And another girl I went out with, Julia Atkinson. I looked around, eyes wide, as though I was in Aladdin's cave. I was only eight years old and I'd never seen so many beautiful women in my life.

'I'm going to like it here,' I thought.

Chapter Two
Corona Academy

My mother gave up the guest house in St Mary's Avenue and moved down to London with me. My father and brothers were left behind to live with friends in Harrogate. People sometimes ask me what dad did for a living. All I ever knew was that he was a malting manager. He used to work for a firm called R & W Paul Ltd. One day he took me to work with him. We went to this huge oast house just outside Pannal near Harrogate. He walked into the warehouse, picked up some malt, sniffed it and said, 'That's fine,' then we jumped back into his Hillman and he dropped me home. For years I thought that was all there was to it. That he would just go in and smell malt.

Mum and I lived in a little rented house in East Ham. For the first few weeks she took me every day to Corona on the District Line Tube. Eventually she weaned me away from depending on her. She would put me in one compartment and sit in the next so that I could see her. That way she would accompany me to school, and meet me afterwards, Then she would be two compartments away, and so on, until eventually one day I looked and she wasn't there. I was on my own.

They were good those early days at Corona Academy. There was Richard O'Sullivan, Francesca Annis, Dennis Waterman and Susan George (not a bad year to be joining a stage school). Of course, as in most schools of the fifties and sixties, we were terrified of the principal, Miss Rona Knight. Everybody was scared to death of her, and of her sister, Miss Muriel, who used to teach us tap dancing. With her stockings rolled down around her ankles and her skirt hoisted up over her knees, she would shuffle, hop, step, shuffle, hop, step.

'No, no, no. You're getting it all wrong!' she would bark, and it would be a smack round the back of the legs. 'You-Have-Not-Learnt-The-Rou-Tine-Yet!'

It was a wonderful spur. Years later I worked with one of my old school chums, Larry Dann, who was Sgt Alec Peters in *The Bill*. We did pantomime together in Lincoln – I was playing the good robber, he the bad.

We looked at each other one day during the rehearsals and said, 'Do you remember the First Routine?'

We did. On the spot we performed the First, the Second, the Third and the Fourth Routines. Hayley, our choreographer at Lincoln, was amazed.

'How do you remember that?' Hayley asked.

'It was hard-wired into us by Miss Muriel,' we said.

That fear of getting it wrong was still with us after all those years.

Rona Knight owned the school. She was even more terrifying than Miss Muriel. She also owned a formidable voice.

When she shouted, 'STOPPPP!!!' in the playground, whatever you were doing, you stopped. The whole playground would be a freeze-frame. Who would be for the high-jump? You certainly took notice of Miss Knight. Perhaps that is the trouble with schools today, that there is no discipline, no fear of the teachers, And fear is not always a bad thing.

Oh, we used to misbehave, like most kids, we would play truant – especially from ballet class – but the fear of being caught was what gave bunking its excitement. It was definitely more fun if the element of death hung over the transgressor, if the stakes were higher.

The average day at Corona went like this: during the morning we would have conventional schooling for three hours – reading, writing and arithmetic. In the afternoons we had our theatrical education depending on the grade we were in. One might have ballet on Monday afternoon, tap on Tuesday, play-reading on Wednesday, Shakespeare on Thursday, and so on.

Most of us weren't very fond of ballet at Corona. Little boys tend not to be keen on wearing tights and jockstraps. The girls loved it, of course, but the boys were much happier skiving off to a little coffee bar called Hernando's Hideaway, named after a song in *The Pajama Game*.

We had a couple of narrow squeaks. There was one afternoon that Jeremy Bulloch, Stewart Guidotti and I bunked off to Hernando's during ballet class. When we came back, we threw our school bags over the wall. I jumped up to follow them, and there, in the playground, picking up the bags was Miss Knight. I jumped back down again.

'What's up …?' began Jeremy.

19

'Shhh! It's Miss Knight!' I mouthed.

Three little white faces. We're for it now. We realised that we had to look again. Jeremy gave me a bunk up and, heart thumping, I peered over the wall. Miss Knight had gone.

We didn't know what to do about our bags, but we knew what to do about ballet class. We sneaked in at the end of the class, took off our shirts and put our towels out as though we had just finished ballet.

Miss Knight came in to the room and called everybody together. Jeremy, Stewart and I skulked at the back, trying to put off as long as possible the moment of reckoning.

Miss Knight was magisterial and awful.

'I found three bags in the playground this afternoon,' she said and our legs turned to jelly. 'Frazer Hines, Jeremy Bulloch, Stewart Guidotti: step forward.'

This was it then. We were for it. Caught bunking off ballet. A more heinous crime than Cain's murder of Abel. I wondered if our execution would be quick and immediate, or slow and painful.

'Yes, Miss Knight,' we said in unison.

'Now, your parents have paid good money for these bags. I do not want to see them lying around the playground, carelessly abandoned. Here they are. Clean them up. Take them home. And do not let me catch you being careless in this way again. Or …' she said balefully, 'there will be trouble.'

Jeremy, Stewart and I exchanged astonished looks. We couldn't believe our luck. Reprieved!

'Yes, Miss Knight,' we said again.

There was one time we did get caught, though. We had become fond of a little flutter on the horses. The old bloke who ran the local chip shop would put a bet on for us at a betting shop called Betty Weldon's in Chiswick. One Derby day we all went back to my house to watch the race on television – after all, it was only ballet class. I believe I backed the winner, Never Say Die.

We nearly did 'die' the next day.

At assembly Miss Knight stood up. 'Frazer, where were you yesterday?' So she'd noticed that I wasn't in ballet class.

'Uh … I had the dentist.'

She pointed to another boy. 'And you?'

'M … my mother was ill.'

'And you?'

'I was poorly.'

What we didn't know was that half the girls hadn't bothered to turn up either. Out of a class of eighteen there were only four students present.

Miss Knight went round the entire company. Excuse after excuse was offered up: dentists, doctors, granny died, flash flood in Hackney. You name it! After the last feeble excuse Miss Knight looked round the class.

'I know what day it was yesterday. I know who won. I also know the starting price.'

Ah.

'I don't want to expel the lot of you and close down half the school. So I'll let you off this time. But don't let it happen again.'

I looked around at the other pupils and wondered if they were thinking the same as me: that next time we needed better excuses!

When I joined Corona there was a boy there who was a very big child star called Jeremy Spencer. I remember sometimes wondering whether I would one day be another Jeremy Spencer. We all felt that. Later we would dream about becoming another Richard O'Sullivan. Richard was also a very young child film star. We used to look up to him. He always used to get the parts. Whenever we would go for an audition, if Richard was there too we felt there was little point turning up; Richard would get the part.

Another obstacle we encountered was the casting director with a fixed idea.

'How old are you?', he might ask.

'I'm ten, sir.'

'Oh dear, the boy I was looking for is only nine.'

'I was nine last year, sir.'

'No, he's got to be nine now.'

This happened to me so many times. That's why, to this day, I'm always very coy about giving my age. Years later I lost an adult part this way.

I met a friend in the pub who said, 'I was going to cast you as the young lieutenant on this army film, but I was told you were thirty. This lieutenant is supposed to be twenty-four.'

'But you said I looked twenty-four,' I said.

'Yes, you look it, Frazer. But now I know you're really thirty, so you're too old for the part.'

The idea of Corona, of course, was that we were to become theatrical performers, and it was never too soon to begin one's professional career. My first audition for a film came along quite soon.

I met the director, William Fairchild. 'Yes, you'll do,' he said.

I went skipping back to school. 'I'm in a film, I'm in a film!'

Janice Field, one of the girls in my class turned round. 'So what? I've done loads.'

That was one thing about Corona; you were never allowed to get big-headed. Whatever job you got there was always somebody in your class that was doing at least as well, and as I've said, Dennis Waterman was there, as well as Susan George and Francesca Annis. They were all working.

And after all, my first film was hardly the springboard to stardom. I was the four hundred and thirty-fourth citizen in a 1955 picture called *John and Julie*. A crowd scene. Of course, when the film came out the whole family had to go and see it. My uncles and aunts from Scotland all came down to see the première. And sure enough, there, outside Buckingham Palace, was Frazer. With about a thousand others. They all said that they could see me, but there wasn't much to see – just a little boy in a school cap waving in the crowd. Looking back today it had quite a cast: Wilfred Hyde-White, Sid James, Colin Gibson and even Peter Sellers.

I was in a number of crowd scenes before I started getting speaking parts, including John Huston's 1956 film *Moby Dick* with Gregory Peck.

One day my agent, Hazel Malone, sister of Miss Rona and Miss Muriel, who handled the show-business department of the school and who represented others such as the aforementioned Richard O'Sullivan, Susan George, Gretchen Franklin, Diana Dors and Roy Barraclough, was asked if I would audition for a film that a production company called Hammer were producing: *X, The Unknown*. It was one of their early science fiction films, coming after their success with *The Quatermass Xperiment*. It starred Dean Jagger and a very young Anthony Newley.

Well, I got the part. I was to play a little boy called Ian Osborn. Ian and his pal Willie were up from Scotland, so I had to use my Scottish accent. We suspected an old man of turning into a vampire bat at night and so decided to go along and witness him actually doing this. So off we went one night with the film crew to Gerrard's Cross chalk pit in Buckinghamshire. One of my lines was that I had to say to Willie, 'Willie, you go down and see if he turns into a vampire bat. I'll wait for you for three minutes.' And off Willie trotted.

We rehearsed the scene with the director, Leslie Norman, (that's right – Barry Norman's father). It was about two o'clock in the morning when Leslie said, 'Action.'

'Willie, you go down and see if he turns into a vampire bat. I'll wait here for three minutes,' I said.

Just then an owl hooted. I turned to Willie and said, 'Make that two minutes!'

Leslie and the crew fell about. 'Cut, cut, cut. No, that's ruined the take.'

'Oh, I'm sorry Mr Norman. I just had to say it.'

'Don't worry, Frazer, it was funny. In fact, you know what …' You could see Leslie's mind working furiously. 'Keep it in. Obviously the owl won't hoot this time, but say the line, wait for a pause, and we'll dub an owl in later on.'

So when you see *X, The Unknown* you'll hear my cheeky ad-libbing. I never got a writing credit for it, though.

I didn't get to see the film at the time. It was classified 'X' and children weren't allowed in to cinemas to see it. It was only years later, when it appeared on television that I got to see my youthful performance. I was entertaining a young lady at home and boasted that an old film of mine was on the box and should we watch it. We did, and after seeing the film, every time I made a move on her. She would say, 'Ah, weren't you sweet, that little cherubic face …' It completely ruined a night of passion.

It was fun being a child actor, though. Yes, it was acting, but nine times out of ten you were being paid to be a little boy playing at cowboys and Indians.

Another film from this period was called *The Weapon*, starring a boy actor called Jon Whiteley. George Cole was in it as well and I had a scene with him. Also in the film was a great American star, Lizabeth Scott, a beautiful blonde, sexy siren, and I, along with a pal from Corona, had a scene with her. What happened is etched into my mind forever.

Lizabeth came on to the set that day wearing a raincoat. We rehearsed the scene with her a couple of times and then the director, Val Guest, said, 'OK, we'll go for a take now.'

Lizabeth opened her coat and all she was wearing underneath was pink underwear.

I had never seen a woman in her underwear before. My eyes came out on stalks. The two of us stood there drinking in the sight of her. Lizabeth was aware of the effect she was having on us.

She smiled and said in that wonderful husky voice of hers, 'Let's get the scene done before these two boys grow up to be men.'

That was probably my best day's work ever while at Corona.

Around that time I arrived home one day to find that Mum had laid on a big spread.

'What's the party for, Mum?'

'It's your father – he's now a £1000 a year man.'

We felt like millionaires. Nowadays amounts like that just pay the fat cats of industry's cigar bills.

I was getting more and more work but the big break was when Shaun Sutton cast me as Napoleon in a 1957 BBC television serial based on the John Buchan novel called *Hunting Tower*, along with my brother Roy playing Thomas Yownie.

After *Hunting Tower* I became a regular member of the Shaun Sutton TV rep company along with Patrick Cargill, Paul Whitsun-Jones and Nigel Arkwright. The next job he gave me was another serial called *The Silver Sword*, and that really made my name. Until then I had just been that little boy on television but *The Silver Sword* was a true breakthrough. Even today people stop me in the street and say, 'Do you remember that thing you did with the sword?' Of course I do.

It was a story about a family in Warsaw during World War II. They were split up from their parents and my character was Jan, a little tearaway who stole from the

Germans and was befriended by the children. In the end Jan helped them escape to Switzerland and meet their estranged family. Jan was adopted by them all in the last episode. Melvyn Hayes (long before his standout turn as Gunner Gloria in *It Ain't Half Hot Mum*) was in it along with Barry Letts who was an actor long before he directed and produced *Doctor Who*. The original book was written by Ian Serraillier. He died in 1994, but I spoke to his daughter recently. I was flattered to hear her say that my performance as Jan was exactly how Ian had written the character.

Those were the days when people would enjoy their Sunday lunch, wash the dishes and settle down to watch the Sunday afternoon serial on the BBC. And I was in a whole stack of them – *Hunting Tower, The Silver Sword, Run to Earth, Queen's Champion, The Long Way Home*. We even did a version of *Cinderella* with the lovely June Thorburn, who was tragically killed a few years later in a plane crash.

I never seemed to stop working at Corona. I was one of the lucky ones. My mother paid the fees for my first term, but after that my earnings paid my way. And we bought a house in Upney – my mother called it a 'sun-trap house'. I came home from school one day and my mother said, 'Son, we're all very proud of you. You've made your first mortgage payment.' Yes, I was paying for the 'sun-trap house'.

We lived there for two years. I was young and I didn't understand it all at the time, but looking back I realised that my mother was not good with money. Although I was constantly working, we were soon back in rented accommodation in St George's Drive, just off Victoria. Every Friday Mr Duplesis would come round for the rent. I never knew where the money from the 'sun-trap house' went. We later ended up with a bungalow in Canvey Island, and I think I bought that too.

Weekends at Canvey were great. Roy and I learned to ride there. Well in a fashion! Mr Wells, who owned the pony rides stall on the seafront, said 'git on that pony' and off you went. We got free rides at the end of the day if we helped in the stables and led the other kids round the paddock at two and six a go. On the way home Roy and I would ride our bikes to Gifhorn Road, along the cinder tracks. Now, if one pedalled like mad then jammed on the back brake, the rear wheel would lock, spin round and give you the feel of a speedway rider! You'd get the smell of cinders and burning rubber and memories would come flooding back to Saturday nights when mum and dad would take us to the speedway to watch our favourite team, Odsal, at Bradford. To this day, whenever I pass Odsal Top I have the smell of the speedway in my nostrils.

While we were in the rented house, Richard O'Sullivan was going from strength to strength and appearing in lots of films, and my mother would say, 'Richard O'Sullivan bought his mother and father a house. Why don't you do what he's done?'

'Mum, I'm not earning that kind of money. I'm just doing television. He's starring in films.'

But it continued to bother her. If she was ever cross with me she would bring that up. That I hadn't bought her a house like Richard O'Sullivan had bought his parents.

Whenever I am at a dinner party and somebody starts to name-drop, I can usually shut them up by saying, 'When I worked with Charlie Chaplin ...' Before you start to try and figure out how old I must be, let me reassure you that it was not a silent movie!

Chaplin made quite a few talkies, of which one was *A King in New York*, a 1957 film starring Dawn Addams and his son, Michael Chaplin. The plot featured Charlie Chaplin as a king in exile and in one scene he visited a school where, if you were a child prodigy, you were provided with all the material you needed to pursue your art.

My character was a little boy who was something of a young Keith Floyd, a chef. My scene involved me rolling out pastry and making cherry cakes, while singing grand opera and incidentally picking my nose. All the while I was making the holes for the cherries with the digit which had just been up my nose.

I went on the set the first day and found Mr Chaplin there already. He was also in the scene, so that not only was I to be directed by him, but I would appear with him too.

'Young man, what's your name?'

'Frazer Hines, sir.'

'Welcome to the film. I'll explain the scene to you. Do you know "When Stars Are Brightly Shining" from *Tosca*?'

'No, sir.'

'Oh. Well, never mind. This is how I want you to do the scene …' And he proceeded to roll out the pastry, singing the aria. He turned round with the cherry cakes and touched the oven door.

'Oh Christ!' he exclaimed.

He pulled a hanky out of his pocket to open the oven with and stowed the cakes inside.

'Right young feller-me-lad – that's what I want you to do.'

So I got the pastry and rolled it out singing any bit of operatic tune that came to mind. When I had rolled it out, picked my nose and made the holes for the cherries, I turned round and grabbed the oven door and said, 'Oh Christ!'

Everybody stopped dead. There was a moment's awful silence, and then Charlie Chaplin burst out laughing. He came over and put his arm round my shoulders saying, 'No, no, no Frazer. I didn't mean you to exclaim in that manner.'

'But Mr Chaplin; that's what you did.'

'Involuntarily. One of the arc-lights had been leaning on the oven door and when I touched it, it was very hot. I don't, however, want *you* to say, "Oh, Christ!", he said smiling.

'I'm sorry, sir.'

'Not to worry. We'll do the scene again.'

When I got home that night my mother was dying to know how it had all gone.

'How did you get on?'

'I don't know. Mr Chaplin said, did I know "When Stars are Brightly Shining" from *Tosca*.'

'You said yes, of course.'

'Mum. I don't *know* it.'

But my mother, who was very musical, opened her music stool and pulled out the relevant score and played it over and over on the piano.

'Learn it,' she said.

'But I think we've done the scene.'

'Doesn't matter. Learn it.'

So I spent that evening learning the piece. By the time we were finished I knew it backwards. The following day I went to Mr Chaplin.

'Yes, young man?'

'It's Frazer.'

'Ah yes, of course it is, of course it is.'

'I've learnt that song.'

'Song?'

'"When Stars Are Brightly Shining", and I immediately set off on a somewhat breathless rendition.

Mr Chaplin stood there amazed and amused. 'My word, you have been busy.'

'My mother said I should learn it for you. Now we can do it in the scene like you wanted.'

He said, 'Well, I was so pleased with the scene last night when I saw the rushes, and what you sang was entirely appropriate. I'm happy with the scene. But full marks to you, young man, for bothering to learn the piece.'

He was a lovely man to work for, although his son Michael might not agree. Many a time when Charlie was directing Michael in a long scene, he bawled his son out in front of the cast and crew alike. We just prayed that he wouldn't shout at us like that. He was a very hard task-master. One boy missed his cue three times out of carelessness. Mr Chaplin went over to his first assistant director and pointed at the boy saying, 'I don't think we shall be requiring that young gentleman's work on this picture any more.' And with that, he was off the set.

Mr Chaplin turned his attention to me. He was scowling and I thought, 'Oh dear!' Then a smile broke over his face; 'Now then, Frazer. Where were we? Ah yes, today's scene ...'

'Mr Chaplin,' I said.

'Yes?'

'Wouldn't it be a good idea if you took your hat off and put it down, and I got some of this cream that I'm doing for the cakes and I put it in your hat, and you turned your back to me, and I put it on the chair, and you went and sat on it. Wouldn't that be funny?'

I was nine or ten years old. And there I was suggesting business to the king of comedy. Nowadays I go cold thinking of my presumption.

He considered the suggestion. 'Now then, Frazer, what we do is this. We take your idea, yes. But instead of just putting cream into my hat – you decorate the hat like a cake with cream and cherries all over it. Put it on the chair and I'll sit on it … that's when we'll have the comedy! That's what makes people laugh.' Instead of cuffing me round the ear for my cheek, he had listened to this precocious nine-year-old boy.

I've never forgotten how Chaplin listened to me. The trouble with people nowadays is that they get to a certain point in their lives and they stop listening. Chaplin, despite his fame, never stopped listening. Mind you, I think he was glad of a little slapstick. Things like this built courage and confidence, and I am to this day so glad I worked with Chaplin. A legend indeed.

There was one time I went for an audition actually terrified that I might get the part. I didn't want to get it, so naturally I got it. It was my first ever stage production. You weren't really allowed to do stage plays in those days until you were twelve, so I was dreading it, I had done live television, of course, but on stage … well, you can look at the audience. They're looking at you. You can see their faces. They're real.

The play was *The Good Woman of Setzuan* by Bertolt Brecht. In the glittering cast were Dame Peggy Ashcroft (in the days before she became a Dame), George Devine, John Osborne, a very young Peter Wyngarde, many years before he became a household name as the flamboyant Jason King, and Joan Plowright, later to become Lady Olivier.

The first day of rehearsal was hell. I had never had to work with such 'theatre people' before. The word 'luvvies' was not in our vocabulary at the time, so nervous wasn't the word. The grown-ups wanted nothing to do with the little-uns. There was me, another boy from Corona called Norman Forman and two others. George Devine, the director and one of the stars of the show, was fine. I guess he wanted the best out of us. We were playing Chinese boys and every night we had to have our bodies 'bowled up' (that's horrible brown make-up) for the show. We hated it. Peggy Ashcroft became more friendly, I suppose once the show was up and running she could relax a little more.

The play ran for a few weeks at the Royal Court after which it was to be replaced with *The Country Wife*. I thought I was going to be in this play as well, but my contract ended with the end of *The Good Woman of Setzuan*. I wanted to stay on because I was enjoying the live theatre. I was disappointed then, but later in my life I spent a lot of time treading the boards, and playing live theatre has been some of the happiest experiences of my professional life.

Chapter Three
Girls 'n' Cars

It will become clear in the course of this book that my life has been defined by three great passions: acting, horses … and women. No man should have to apologise for loving women. And I have had my fair share – perhaps more than my fair share – of the pleasures of winning women, and the acute pain of losing them. Some of my relationships were important, and some just fun. I wouldn't wish a single one of them away, well maybe one! Arriving at Corona on that first day I may have been dazzled by the casual abundance of beauty, but I was a quick learner. I always have been.

Corona Academy tended to engender a certain precocity in one's approach to the fair sex. At the age of fourteen I was going out with two girls at the same time. One was Julia Atkinson, who I had first laid eyes on the day I arrived at Corona, and with whom I had done a commercial for Butlin's Holiday Camps. We had to run around playing tag. Happy the boy who is obliged for professional reasons to chase around and play with a girl he fancies rotten! The other girl was a blonde called Vicky Harrington, whose father was very well known as one of the leading extras in the film world.

Vicky, though, soon fell out of love with me because I made the mistake of introducing her to Michael Anderson Junior, son of the film director, who was appearing with me in *The Queen's Champion*. They started a relationship which lasted for years. In fact Michael took her back to the states with him and eventually they got married. But I wasn't too upset. I still had Julia and besides there was another girl I rather liked, a Canadian called Jane Ross. I was soon to work with her, alongside my pal Dennis Waterman. It was a play on Granada TV called *The Member of the Wedding* adapted from the novel by Carson McCullers. We were all chaperoned, of course, which was a requirement up to the age of fifteen. A Mrs Callum took us up to Manchester for the recording.

Afterwards we returned to Manchester Piccadilly where we were given first-class sleepers for the journey home. Dennis and I were wildly excited; we leapt into adjacent compartments. 'Yippee!'

But Mrs Callum had met boys like us before. She knew better than to allow us to make our own arrangements.

'No, boys! You will not choose where you sleep. I will decide for you. Jane you go in there. Frazer, you go in that one, and Dennis, that one.

Oh rats! I went into my compartment and sat on the bed with a long face. So much for the prospect of high jinks.

The train pulled away. I stood up and took my jacket off. I opened the wardrobe to hang it up. Only it wasn't a wardrobe. Standing on the other side of the door, and looking very surprised, was Jane. Mrs Callum had inadvertently put us in a family suite, two compartments with a connecting door. We couldn't believe our luck.

'Jane …' I began.

'Shhh!' She said, giggling. 'She'll never know.' And she drew me into her compartment where we settled down to a little kissing and cuddling.

Leaning back on her bunk a little later, playing with Jane's hair and rather enjoying her closeness, I was suddenly seized by a horrible thought.

'Oh my God!'

'What is it?' Jane asked.

'Oh nothing. Forget it.' I smiled at her and reassured her that nothing was wrong.

I had just realised how lucky I had been. I could have opened the door and seen Mrs Callum standing there. I'm awfully glad it was Jane.

I was growing up pretty fast. And when a beautiful, white-haired girl named Jill Haworth joined Corona, I was smitten. I can be forgiven for that. She had the same effect on most of the chaps. We dated two or three times and it looked like we were beginning a serious relationship when she was whisked off by Otto Preminger to make the film *Exodus* with Paul Newman and Sal Mineo, and after that she stayed in America. I never saw her again. She was one of the might-have-beens. Showbusiness can be cruel like that, it will throw you together with someone wonderful for a brief period and then snatch her away again. You learn to be philosophical about it. I have since spoken to Jill and she's invited me to come over and see her in New York, where she now lives.

There were light moments, though, professionally and romantically. Jeremy Bulloch, Gareth Tandy, and another member of the gang, John Pike, and I got to play in a 1960 series for the Children's Film Foundation called *The Young Jacobites*. We all flew up to Inverness Airport in an old Dakota, and then took a coach to Dunvegin, where we were filming on the lovely island of Skye. It was like being paid to go and play with your pals, Also in the serial was a beautiful Corona girl I mentioned previously, Francesca Annis.

We all fancied Francesca like mad, but she would have none of it. We got the impression she thought she was far too good for this rabble.

Our chaperone, Mrs Seaborn, unfortunately suffered a bereavement halfway through the shoot and she had to go back to England. We were four days without a chaperone before she was replaced.

Francesca was being highly superior with us, and the crew were fawning all over her, bringing her coffee and paying court. So we decided to send her to Coventry. We wouldn't speak to her at all. The director, John Reeve, pleaded with us to stop it. We were swines.

'Nothing in our contract says we have to speak to her except on set.'

Fifteen year old kids speaking like that!

Eventually we made a pact, John, Jeremy, Gareth and I.

'Francesca,' we said one night, 'we will speak to you … if you give us all a kiss.'

'Oh no. Do I have to?'

'Otherwise we won't speak to you …'

So she gave us all a kiss with her beautiful soft lips and from then on, not only did we speak to her, but I think we all fell in love with her as well.

In between jobs we were still taught at Corona. One term I remember we had a method teacher by the name of Mr Jago. Now he really was into the method acting. Just like Marlon Brando, he believed you had to get under the skin of the character. In acting class you were 'trees' or 'be an egg bursting your shell to depict life beginning'. Most of us thought it was a hoot. I mean, after all, we'd done plenty of real jobs by now. I remember he once said to me, 'Frazer, you are a broken and dejected kirby grip. (Yes, I do mean the type girls wear in their hair!). Show me!'

So I went and lay on the floor. After about four minutes he said, 'Great! I could really see the life draining from you – wonderful!' I hadn't the heart to tell him I was having a kip!

Time passed and I was ready for my first car. I was seventeen and held a full driving licence, having passed my test first time. However, I was the last of my gang at Corona to pass. Oh, the humiliation if I'd failed. I saved up like mad and for the princely sum of £10 I bought a Wolseley Hornet sports car. It was a two-seater with a big leather belt across the bonnet to keep it on. Actually, I had shared an earlier car with my brother, Roy, an old Morris 10/4, which looked like something Al Capone would have driven, but the Hornet was mine. And like your first girl, your first car is special. I used to love driving to Corona in it with my hair blowing in the wind: I felt like a million dollars.

I loved it right up until my first accident. There was bound to be one, although this one wasn't my fault. By this time I was in the student branch of Corona which meant that I had finished with the conventional lessons in the morning. It was acting, and dancing and Shakespeare full-time from then onwards. School uniform was no longer required, we could wear civvies.

I was giving a lift home to Chris Edie (who later went on to join the New Vaudeville Band).

'I can smell burning,' Chris said, then he looked out at the side of the car. 'Look at the engine!'

Through the slats in the bonnet I could see flames. We were on fire. The faster I drove, the fiercer the flames were. What to do? I was afraid that if I stopped it might blow up. I switched the petrol off. Chris and I looked at each other as we raced forward.

'We've got to bail out,' I said.

So we bailed out. We had just come from stage-fall class, so we were well practised in landing without hurting ourselves.

The car careened on. As we picked ourselves up the car jumped the kerb and hit a bus-stop. There were two ladies waiting there, so busy gossiping with each other that they hardly noticed the impact.

'The car's going to blow up!' I shouted at them.

'What, dear?'

'It's going to blow up!'

'What is?'

'The car!'

'Oh look, there's a car on fire ... Oh my gawd ...' and they took to their heels.

I ran to a call-box, dialled 999, and waited for the fire brigade to arrive. By this time, because I had switched off the petrol, the last flickers of flame were dying. The fire brigade arrived and hosed the car down. It was a forlorn sight, my lovely Wolseley Hornet, all soaked in water.

What had happened was that the carburettor hose had come loose and fallen onto the cylinder head, which is very hot. So the hose had melted. All the petrol pumped from the fuel tank was spilling over the cylinder head where it ignited. By switching the petrol off I had averted an explosion.

I got the car fixed and restored to its former glory, but I never felt good about it again, and I sold it very soon afterwards.

I bought my next car from my brother Roy. It was a 1949 MG TC, and I will always associate it with a girl I met the very first day I took it to school. You know how you don't notice somebody, and then when you do, you can't imagine how you missed them? I brought my new red car to Corona and went to the coffee bar. I sat down, looked across the room and there was a girl sat two tables away. She looked like a young Elizabeth Taylor. I went over and asked her what class she was in.

'I'm in the class just below yours.'

'What's your name?'

'Ann Davies.'

We got talking and I wondered how long she had been at Corona. 'About two years,' Ann said.

How had I not noticed her before? She was stunning. I asked her out that night and we went for supper. I drove her back to her parents' house in Ladbroke Grove in my red MG. Her father was a stockbroker and her mother was a retired English movie actress. They were asleep when we got back and Ann invited me in for coffee. She wanted me to hear a new record she had bought. It was 'Deep Purple' by Nino Tempo and April Stevens. We danced to it and it felt really good. So we put the record back on and danced some more.

'Do you have a boyfriend,' I asked holding her close.

'No. Do you have a girlfriend?'

'No.'

My previous girlfriend, Sandy, had dropped me so I was free.

We played the record again and again and kissed by the firelight. It was the beginning of a wonderful three-year relationship. Whenever I hear 'Deep Purple' I think of Ann.

Ann's parents were lovely people and were always encouraging me to marry her. At the time I wasn't thinking about settling down, though, and I said 'no'. Katherine, her mother, even offered to settle a thousand pounds a year on us, which was a lot of money in those days. You could almost live on it! But I didn't want to take money for marrying a girl, not even one as beautiful as Ann.

We often went out as a foursome with a friend of Ann's, a girl called Sally Bulloch (Jeremy's sister), and a friend of mine, Mike Randle, who was boarding with me and my parents. Mike's dad was a doctor down south and it was too far for him to commute every day. We would go out in my car and pull into a lay-by for a kiss and cuddle, all four of us. The plastic windows at the back would get all steamed up and the glass windscreen would also steam up. We were happy the way teenagers have always been happy in cars. I still marvel that Michael and Sally contrived to get in the back of a two-seater MG where the suitcase normally goes, and I am lost in admiration that they were able so much as to breathe let alone canoodle. There are few things in nature less easily discouraged than youthful ardour.

Nearly eighteen, my horizons were beginning to broaden. My brothers had both left home. Much to my mother's chagrin, Roy was living and working with a bookmaker and his family in Ealing; he was going out with their daughter, Jackie. Iain had upset the applecart by marrying a Maltese girl and was working over in Hamburg at the Top Ten Club. I was dying to visit him and eventually I did.

I walked into the Top Ten and there was Iain and his boss Peter Eckhorn waiting for me.

Peter put out his hand, 'Frazer – you are Iain's brother. I've heard so much about you. What would you like?' He waved his hand towards the bar.

I was in a mischievous mood, so out of bravado I said, How about a bottle of Wild Turkey?' This was a brand of straight bourbon whiskey which I had heard a lot about but never tried.

'Wild Turkey for you. Your birthday's coming up, isn't it?' He reached over the bar and plonked the bottle in front of me. Peter insisted that we all toast my arrival, and then Iain took me upstairs to the bedrooms. They were the grottiest, filthiest accommodation I have ever seen.

Iain must have seen me turn my nose up at it because he put his arm round me and said, 'You know the Beatles played here, at the Top Ten?'

'Yes, of course.' Everybody knew about the Beatles and their all-night marathons in Hamburg.

'This is John and Paul's room,' said Iain.

For the entire week I spent in Hamburg I never saw daylight. There was a group playing at the club called The League of Gentlemen. They started playing at 7 pm and finished around 2 am. After that we would all go round the corner to the Mango Shanky for a *schweinekotelett und kartoffeln* – a pork chop and potatoes – and a beer, wine, brandy and then back to the Top Ten to sleep the day away.

One night Iain took me down to the Herbertstrasse, which was the street where the prostitutes lived and worked. I had never seen anything like it in my life! There, in all the windows, were these girls in advanced states of undress. They were all sitting on cushions. I asked Iain why.

'Each cushion represents five marks. So that girl over there, sitting on two cushions, she would cost you ten marks to sleep with her.'

Sleep with a prostitute! I couldn't think of anything less appealing. There were some distinctly unprepossessing ones sitting on just three feathers.

'What does she charge? Three pfennigs?'

I was just seventeen on that trip, and it was an education to wander around the Herbertstrasse on the Reeperbahn.

The League of Gentlemen were a good bunch. Every night I sat in the front row with a couple of beers, and they would let me get up with them and join in a sort of bluesy number called 'Humpty Dumpty'. They would tip me the wink and I would jump up on stage, grab a tambourine, and sing my couple of verses.

There was a girl sort of hanging around who they called Hammersmith because she came from Hammersmith. I found her a little depressing; she seemed to have no life of her own. She just waited for one of the men to select her and then she would be his for as long as he wanted her. I came to associate her with the nightly squeals of delight and moans of pleasure from the many and various bedrooms upstairs at the Top Ten. When she learned that I was Iain's younger brother and that I was an actor who had appeared in various shows she had heard of, she wanted to get to know me. But I thought of her extreme availability and decided that I didn't want to know her any better than I already did.

I was young and inexperienced. But word soon got around that this young English actor was in town, so I learnt a little German from my brother. '*Ich bin ein junger Englischer schauspieler, komme mit mir zu meinem schlafzimmer ...*' (I am a young English actor, come with me to my bedroom). It may not be one of the all-time great chat-up lines, but I was soon surrounded by a bevy of German beauties, mainly because I bought them all *schweinekotelett und kartoffeln*.

There was a recording studio at the Top Ten Club and while I was

38

in Hamburg, Iain, his resident group and I actually made a couple of records: a cover version of the Beatles' 'I Feel Fine', which I was told got to number one in the German hit parade, and also Yardbirds' 'Heart Full Of Soul'. We made them in the spirit of the times and I wish I could find a copy of those records now.

I celebrated my eighteenth birthday in Hamburg. I did it with my usual routine – into the Top Ten, drank a couple of beers, sang 'Humpty Dumpty' with The League of Gentlemen and popped round the corner at 2 am for *schweinekotelett*.

As the night turned into morning, Iain said, 'It's getting light. I've got a present for you.' He took me outside on to the deserted Hamburg street as the first rays of dawn began to touch the tops of the buildings on the western side of Reeperbahn, and there by the pavement was a big American Packard. 'Happy birthday, Frazer.'

'You've bought me a *car*?'

'No, idiot. Your present's *inside* the car.'

He opened the Packard door and I got in, and there was this German girl. I thought I recognised her. It was one of Iain's girlfriends. And, if it is not indelicate to relate, her address was in the vicinity of Herbertstrasse.

'What's the idea, Iain?'

'She's your present, Frazer. She's going to teach you everything I know.' And with that he slammed the door and the car set off up the road at a terrific speed. I could hear Iain laughing. I looked back at him pressing my startled little face up against the window.

The car pulled up at some traffic lights and I wrestled the door open and threw myself out, rolling over and over on the pavement. I had no plans to get intimate with a prostitute, thank you very much. Apart from any considerations of my dignity, I had heard lurid tales of venereal diseases and I couldn't dismiss from my imagination visions of suppurating sores. But my main objective was one of pride. Commercial sex was just something I didn't do.

I picked myself up and dashed back to Iain. He had guessed at some of the reasons for my reluctance.

'Don't worry about the girl,' he said. 'They're safe in Germany. They have regular checks at clinics. Come on, Frazer. You've got to start sometime …'

I ran past him back to the Top Ten and straight up to my room. I leapt into bed and hid under the covers.

What Iain didn't know was that I didn't need his help to lose my virginity. I had disposed of it five years earlier in Canvey Island on a dyke with a girl called Janet. (There's no need for that silly giggling; back then the only meaning the word 'dyke' had was a sea wall). Janet and I had met on occasions when my family had gone down to our bungalow and we often hung out together. One day we were out walking on the sea wall and we sat down talking and giggling. Playfully we started wresting and we rolled down the hill … and that was it. This seemed to go there and that seemed to fit there. And that was that. My first close encounter of any kind.

Anyway! When I returned from Hamburg in 1964 I was asked to play the part of John Trenchard, the young hero in a BBC production of *Moonfleet*. But at the time the BBC also had a show on called *Moonstrike*, all about a Lysander air crew working with the French Resistance. So, *Moonfleet* was changed to *Smuggler's Bay*. It was to be directed by Christopher Barry and also in the cast was John Phillips playing Elzevir Block and Patrick Troughton as Ratsey. It was set in the seventeenth century so I had long hair with a P J Proby bow at the back, breeches, a waistcoat, frock coat and buckle shoes. I love wearing those romantic costumes and I felt wonderful in that part. I have liked romantic costumes since I was a boy; early on at Corona I was cast as the leader of a group of boy bandits in the 1958 TV series *William Tell* with Conrad Phillips as Tell. (Working with Conrad was a joy; he was such a nice man. Years later we worked together again when he played my boss Christopher Meadows in *Emmerdale Farm*.) My costume in *William Tell* included great big boots and a little sword. I so enjoyed clumping around the studio corridors in those boots that the wardrobe department used to tease me about it: 'Here comes Frazer in his important boots!'

Also in the cast was Derren Nesbitt, playing the Landburger's henchman.

Years later I was working with Derren at the Theatre Royal in Windsor and he swore blind we were of the same age. The next day was a matinee and after the first performance I called all the cast into the green room and showed my episode of *William Tell*, 'The Boy Slaves', and in one particular scene there was this very grown up lieutenant played by Derren bullying a little cherubic-faced yours truly!

'Now then Derren,' I said. 'We are the same age?'

'Got me, you little bastard!' he said.

We were to start filming *Smuggler's Bay* at Ealing Studios and then go on location to a beautiful spot at Lulworth Cove in Dorset. About four days before we were due to start, I was round at Ann's house in Ladbroke Grove with Michael and a couple of friends. I went into the kitchen to get a glass of water and as I was coming back out in to the garden the wind caught the kitchen door. I put my hand up instinctively to stop the door, but my hand went straight through the pane of glass.

There was blood everywhere. I reeled round. My middle finger was hanging by a strip of skin. Ann took one look and almost fainted. Luckily Michael was a doctor's son.

'Quick give him brandy,' he said.

He grabbed my hand and put it under the cold tap, applying his thumb to try and staunch the flow of blood. Ann came back with the brandy. She took another look at me bleeding freely into the sink and drank the brandy herself.

Ann rang for an ambulance; in those days before government cut-backs it was an excellent service. Today they seem to want patients to fit in with the Health Service instead of the other way round. We're supposed to know better than to take a heart condition to Hammersmith, we should have the foresight to be ill in Manchester. Happily, I was bleeding to death in a different era. Within five minutes the ambulance arrived, and I was whisked away to hospital.

A doctor put me back together again. He stitched my three fingers up. He fed my middle finger back onto the bone and stitched round it. He has saved my finger, but it now had three huge bandages, great finger stalls like I had a bunch of bananas for a hand.

'Will I be able to work?' I asked.

'Oh no, my lad. Three months off for you. At least.' I think he thought he was doing me a favour. An excuse for three months off work.

'But I have to work.'

'Yes, yes, good lad. But it can't be helped. I'm signing you off for three months.' He thought I was being conscientious.

Michael took the doctor to one side. 'He really does have to work. He's got a job starting next week.'

'He won't have to.'

'He wants to. He's an actor. He's starting a new TV show.'

'Oh.' It finally dawned on the old boy. He actually gave some thought to the possibility. 'Well I'm not sure if he will be able to.'

I got home that night and the anaesthetic began to wear off. Boy, it hurt! At about two in the morning I felt as though somebody had squeezed my fingers with pliers. My hand was throbbing very badly. I switched the light on and saw that the bandage was getting darker and darker. The white bandage on my middle finger had turned entirely scarlet.

I dashed into Michael's room and roused him. 'Michael, I think I'm bleeding to death.'

He put his glasses on and had a look, but the bleeding seemed to have stopped. For an hour Michael and I sat on the end of his bed watching my finger to see if the bleeding started again. The blood turned black as it dried. But the bleeding had stopped.

In the morning I went back to the hospital where they were very accommodating. Except for the nurse who treated me.

'It hurts like hell, nurse.'

'I'm sure it does. Well, I shall have to cut the bandage off. Put your hand on the table.'

Instead of cutting my bandage away from the stitches, this nurse put her scissors in right next to the stitches in my finger. 'Nurse, the stitches …!'

'Don't tell me my job.' The nurse clipped away and turned round to chat to a friend and she contrived to jab the scissors into the open wound where I had stitches. I fairly hit the roof.

'Don't be such a baby,' she said.

Another nurse came in to see what the row was about.

'He won't have the bandage taken off.'

The second nurse took the first one aside: 'You're supposed to soak the bandage before you cut it off.'

'Oh, it's not such a big thing. I'll have it off in a jiffy.'

The second nurse took over. She brought a bowl of medicated solution and soaked the bandage in it, The bandage became soft and she gently turned my hand over and cut the material off. She repaired the stitches where they had come loose in the night and rebandaged me.

I went home more comfortable, but still worried. I was afraid that I was going to lose my job.

Filming began the next day and in some trepidation I drove down to Ealing. I had sold my beloved MG by then for £110; I traded it in for a red Triumph Herald drop-head four-seater. I bought this on the strength of the money I was going to earn from working on *Smuggler's Bay*. I could see me having to give it back.

I went into the studio holding my bad hand behind my back. Chris Barry was there with the rest of the crew. With a heavy heart I said, 'Chris, I've got something to tell you. I've had a little accident.'

'Like what?'

I showed him my hand.

'Oh my God! What are we going to do?'

Chris and his assistant, Michael E Briant, who later went on to work with me in both *Doctor Who* and *Emmerdale Farm*, went into a huddle and came up with nothing. Everybody started to chip in ideas – we could put something over his fingers to hide the gleaming white of the bandages … we could paint them to look like something else.

The studio nurse said we couldn't paint them because there might be toxins in the paint that could get into my bloodstream.

Andy, the prop man came up with an idea. 'Guv, I've got a packet of three in my pocket – can't we try those?'

It seemed worth a try. Andy rolled the condoms over my fingers. It didn't look very convincing but it was a rich source of humour for wags on the sets as I wandered around with three prophylactics on my fingers.

'If you think I'm acting with these things on my fingers, you've got another think coming,' I said.

Eventually the wardrobe mistress cut the fingers off some heavy duty brown gloves. We slipped those over my fingers and taped them to my hand. The first scene required John Trenchard to explore an old mausoleum. I spent two days carrying a lantern as I explored the graves and crypts. The character became left handed of necessity, and the offending right hand was held down out of sight at his side. If they ever repeat that series, have a look – you'll see that John Trenchard's right hand is not in shot very often at all.

Ann was desperate to settle down and start a family, and I was still not ready to do that. So we went our separate ways. Years later, when I got divorced from Gemma Craven, she was living in Canada, and she had just got divorced too. She read about my divorce in a magazine, and rang my agent to see if I still remembered her. Of course I did. She invited me to go over to Canada and stay with her for a few days. She met me at the airport with her chauffeur – she had become a successful businesswoman – and there she was, as beautiful and as reminiscent of the young Elizabeth Taylor as ever. Standing beside her was a tall Canadian boy who turned out to be Charles, her son, and a lovely daughter called Katherine after Ann's mum.

I had a marvellous time. My four days turned into seven, then nine. One day when we were out having a picnic, big, blond, athletic Charles looked at Ann and said, 'Mom, do you know something? If you'd married Frazer I'd be little and dark.'

It was a provocative observation. Ann and I were getting on so well. We even talked about picking up the pieces and carrying on where we had left off so many years ago. But my career was in Britain and her business was in Canada. She wondered about selling her business and coming over to England. She did come over to visit and started looking at schools for Katherine and Charles. We even looked at a few houses. Then she went back to Canada, and in the course of several transatlantic phone calls we realised that for her to start her business from scratch in England would be impossible, and it would be equally impossible for me to go to Canada and try and get work in television and film there. We decided quite amicably that it was best if she stayed there and I stayed in England. But we are still great friends to this day.

That is one of the aspects of my life in which I take satisfaction. I count myself lucky with women. I have known a large number and have been privileged to be romantically involved with some of the most beautiful in England. And I believe I could call any one of them and go to lunch or supper. I don't take any credit for this, but I seem to have the knack for staying good friends with my ex-lovers.

There are a couple of exceptions of course, and we shall be coming to them in due course.

Chapter Four
Meeting My Doctor

I was swinging in the sixties in Chiswick at 44 Grosvenor Road – the upstairs flat in a house. Not long after my Hamburg trip Iain had got divorced and obtained custody of his two boys, Shaun and Clive. His daughter stayed with her mother but Shaun and Clive came to live with Mum and Dad and myself, and we found ourselves bringing them up while Iain stayed abroad. This made it rather cramped at Grosvenor Road, but life was fun, particularly when my father was around.

Dad was a very shy person really. Where my mother was noisily proud of me, Dad didn't like ostentatious expressions of approval. My mother would announce, 'Frazer's on TV tonight!' and he would make some excuse: he had to go out; he was expected somewhere else. But there would be times when he would stay while the family watched a performance of mine in a darkened room, and when he thought no one could see, there would be a little tear in his eye. He was the same about the theatre. He would find excuses not to come when Mum and all the family came to see me in a show. But once when I was appearing with Bernard Lee ('M' in all those James Bond films) and Kathleen Harrison in a West End Show called *Norman* at the Duchess Theatre, he sneaked in to the back of the auditorium and saw the play.

He had a wonderful dry sense of humour. My mother enjoyed a laugh as much as anybody, but I think I get my own sense of fun from my Dad. His handle at work was 'Joke-A-Minute Hines'. One night we went mob-handed to see my pal Dennis Waterman in *The Music Man* in the West End. We sat down expectantly waiting for curtain up, when a man and his wife came past. So we all stood up in our seat to let them through. But once we were all nicely settled the man stood up, and we had to stand up again while he shuffled past us. He came back with a programme and we were all able to sit down. He got up again. 'Excuse me, excuse me …' He came back with a box of chocolates and sat down. After a couple of minutes he got up again and off he went. *What is it this time?* He came back with an ice-cream. My father tapped him on the shoulder. 'Do you know, sir, I'm so glad you didn't bring your golf clubs with you.' And we all fell about laughing.

There was a serious side to my father too. He was very well informed on a wide variety of subjects. He might tell you about the private life of a forgotten nineteenth century prime minister one minute, and be describing in detail the best route to Colchester the next. He was also very political, and in fact had ambitions to enter local politics. He became a Liberal candidate in Chiswick, and overcame his shyness to go knocking on doors to explain the minutiae of Liberal policies to the voters. I used to go around with him, hoping that a face off the telly would help. It is irrational, but people will welcome a famous face into their homes much more happily than one they have never seen before. I regret to say that I didn't seem to help him much. He didn't get in.

Iain was still working at the Top Ten Club in Hamburg, so I was a sort of surrogate father to Shaun and Clive. I didn't want them to miss out on the things Iain would have done for them. I remembered the kind of big brother he had been to me and Roy, the way he used to frighten us after seeing *The Wolf Man* at the pictures. So if Shaun and Clive were watching a late-night horror movie on TV, I would make excuses and go upstairs to bed. We had a coat-stand on the landing and I would hide in the cloaks. As Shaun and Clive came upstairs after the film, saying, 'Wasn't it creepy? No wonder Uncle Frazer went to bed early …', the coat-stand would attack them and they would run shrieking to bed.

On the work front I was appearing in an ITV children's serial called *No Man's Island*, directed by Cecil Petty. Jennifer Tafler, daughter of actor Sidney Tafler, was in it and also it starred Vincent Ball.

This was an adventure serial about a canoe club on the Thames which kept coming across bank robbers and smugglers. The gimmick was that we spent our time in kayaks, little Eskimo canoes. For the part I had to learn to paddle and turn upside down and right myself, and to this day I can handle a canoe pretty well. But I did nearly drown one day. We were shooting a scene in a canal and some very kind person opened a lock gate without notifying us. A torrent of water came thundering down and turned me over. Now, all our training had been in a swimming pool where the water is clear and fairly still. This was a very different experience. I was trapped, holding my breath under water, while the kayak buffeted along. You are held in the canoe by a sort of frock that stops the water getting in to the boat. Eventually I did kick myself free and get righted, coughing and spluttering, and made for the bank, holding on to the props so that they didn't get lost.

Cecil was waiting at the canal bank. 'You silly bugger! What about all those lessons you had in the swimming pool?'

'Cecil, the swimming pool is a mill pond compared with this.'

'Bring the kayak in,' said Cecil, 'I'll show you how to get in and out of a canoe without falling out of it.'

He stepped in to the canoe, gesturing with his hands as if to say, 'You see? It's all a question of smooth actions.' As he slid his bottom into the kayak over he went, upside down in the canal. We all watched. A Peter Stuyvesant cigarette surfaced, which was Cecil's preferred brand. An arm appeared for a moment, thrashing madly.

I looked at the first assistant. 'I think he's drowning,' I said.

'I think you're right. We'd better help.'

'Let's give him another five minutes.'

'No, I think we'd better rescue him.'

'Oh all right.' I jumped back in and righted the canoe. Cecil came up spluttering.

'So that's how it's done!' I said.

'Don't be cheeky!'

Cecil cropped up again a couple of years later in 1964. He was now producing *Emergency Ward 10* and he wanted me for the show.

Thus I found myself driving down to Elstree Studios one morning in my little sports car with the hood down to play the part of Tim Birch, a medical student with unfortunate condition of fulminating ulcerative colitis. Once you've learnt to say a phrase like that, you never forget it!

Emergency Ward 10 was one of the top rated shows of the day. So I walked in to the rehearsal room full of trepidation. I was surrounded by stars – John Carlisle, Paula Byrne, Desmond Carrington, Jill Browne. My heart was in my mouth until Paula Byrne came over to me.

'Hello, you must be Frazer. I'm Paula Byrne. Welcome to the show.'

'I know who you are,' I stammered.

Desmond Carrington, came over and introduced himself, and one by one all the stars welcomed me to the show. Jill Browne brought me a cup of coffee. I said to myself then, 'If ever I do a long-running television series, whenever a new person joins the cast I shall do that too.' It's miserable to come in to an established cast who all know each other and be ignored on your first day. Ever since then I've tried to be as welcoming to new colleagues as the cast of *Emergency Ward 10* were to me.

The studio was at Highbury and television was live in those days. This was a pretty hairy way of making programmes. We filmed an episode one day in an operating theatre after which I had a scene where I was recuperating. I had to get from one scene to the next pretty sharpish. During the operating scene I had my eyes closed with the oxygen mask on. John Carlisle was massaging my tummy, pretending to operate, murmuring his lines, and I nodded off. I actually fell asleep!

The next thing I knew my dresser was shaking me, hissing, 'Frazer, Frazer, wake up!'

'Where am I?'

'In the studio. You're needed for the next scene in the hospital bed. Come on!' He dragged me off the operating table, stripping my gown off as we went, putting me into my pyjamas, and threw me into the bed. He pulled up the blankets and skipped out of shot just as the cameras cut to me.

I was half asleep, but I was supposed to be coming round from an operation anyway. I played the scene like that. Cecil said afterwards, 'You know, Frazer, that was really wonderful. I really believed that you were drowsy and disorientated.'

Later in the run the shows were recorded. The studios were quite small and the same set had to be Men's Surgical Ward and, with a little judicious set redressing, the Women's Medical Ward. I would leap out of bed and it would be occupied by another actor. One day I was sharing a bed with a little Filipino girl on this basis, and I thought it would be fun if I didn't vacate it on cue. She dashed on to the set and jumped into the bed, and I popped my head over the covers.

'Hi there, how lovely to see you.'

She shrieked like she'd seen a ghost. In those days a man and women in bed together was scandalous.

I'm often asked who it was that gave me my first screen kiss. Well it was on *Emergency Ward 10*. My character was in love with Nurse Kate Ford played by Jane Rossington (who went on to star as Jill Harvey in *Crossroads* in 1981). In the show I sneaked out of bed and ran over to the nurses' quarters. I stood under Nurse Kate's window and sang 'All My Loving' (by the Beatles). She ran down and opened the door in her nightdress (that's a funny place to have a door) and we kissed. I've met her many times since and we always reminisce about our first kiss together.

Richard Thorp had left *Emergency Ward 10* to appear in his own show *Oxbridge 2000*, but he joined *Emmerdale* years later. Richard and I used to laugh about the *Emergency Ward 10* days when he used to receive 2,500 fan letters a week, not one of them written by himself!

They asked me to stay on in *Emergency Ward 10*. Tim Birch would graduate from medical student to doctor. But at the time I didn't want to get tied to a long-running series. I was still young and ambitious and had my sights set on being a film star. So I turned it down.

And anyway I was never short of work. Straight out of *Emergency Ward 10* I played a farmer's son in an ITV sitcom about a naval base starring Anton Rodgers – the name escapes me. My agent, Hazel Malone, used to say, 'Frazer you've got a horseshoe face.' I went from one job to another. Hazel sent me during the lunch-hour of the sitcom to Wardour Street where I had an audition for a film. In my costume as a country farm-boy I dashed over to Wardour Street. The casting director took one look at me and said, 'Oh, no, no, no. I'm afraid you've wasted your time. I'm looking for a gang leader … but you … no, you don't look right.'

'Before you go any further,' I said. 'You have to know that this is not *my* tweed suit.'

'It doesn't matter. You don't look like a gang leader.'

'Look, there's a BBC wardrobe label in the back of the jacket … They plastered my hair down for the part … I'm in character. I could look like your gang leader.'

'I'm sorry, uh … Frazer, isn't it? It's just not on.'

Crestfallen I left. I rang Hazel and told her all about it.

'Never mind dear,' she answered sympathetically. 'Another day, eh?'

At the end of the week I had finished the sitcom, and I was at home when the phone rang.

'Hello, darling. It's Hazel. That audition you went for the other day – they still haven't cast it so I'm putting you forward again.'

'Hazel, they've seen me and they didn't want me.'

'Listen, darling, listen. They only vaguely remember seeing you. This time jazz yourself up for the part, darling.'

I put on my leather jacket, tight jeans, and a pair of cowboy boots that I had bought on a trip to New York with my mother. I think I must have been one of the first people in England to wear cowboy boots.

So there I was outside the casting director's office, looking much more like a gang leader in my black leather jacket and sharp American boots. I kicked the door open. I had failed to get the part once already, so I had nothing to lose. I threw myself casually into a chair and put my boots on the table. 'Nah, then John. Wot's this part all abaht?'

The casting director was thrilled. 'I don't have to look any further. You are Tony. You are the part!' Suddenly his brow furrowed. 'Hang on, haven't I seen you before …?'

'Well, John, you might 'ave seen me on the box. I done quite a bit o' work.'

'Perfect.'

I pulled out a flick-knife that Iain had brought me back from Germany and started cleaning my nails with it. 'So when do we start?'

'Keep that in, I love it!'

I learned something from that experience. You should avoid as much as possible asking a casting director to use his imagination. You'd think it was a casting director's job to look beyond the surface to see the material he has to work with, but if he wants to cast a soldier, get yourself a short haircut.

After filming for whatever this was – again the title of the production escapes me – I was at home for only a couple of days before Hazel rang me again. 'You've got to go and see Innes Lloyd at the BBC for a part in *Doctor Who*.'

I was very excited: *Doctor Who* was one of the great successes of the day. Although it was a children's programme it was very prestigious and well thought of. William Hartnell was playing the Doctor as a sort of absent minded professor.

Innes Lloyd was a charming man.

'Hallo, Frazer old boy,' he said with his pipe in his mouth. 'Shaun Sutton told me I should have a look at you. We're doing a four-episode story concerning Highlanders, and Shaun tells me you're very handy with a Scots' accent.'

'I *am* half Scots.'

'So do you fancy playing Jamie?'

'Well yes, but don't you want me to read for it?'

'No, that'll be all right.'

A few days later I went for my costume fitting and found myself up at Frensham Ponds which periodically doubles as Germany, Switzerland, Austria, Scotland and anywhere else in the world that the BBC required it to be. I had spent time there many years earlier, traipsing around being Napoleon for Shaun Sutton in John Buchan's *Hunting Tower* and also Jan in *The Silver Sword*.

Just before I started on the show, Patrick Troughton had taken over from William Hartnell as the Doctor. I had worked with him before. He had played one of the smugglers on *Smuggler's Bay*.

'I see your hand has cleared up,' he said when we first met. What a memory! He looked at my three fingers which had been nearly severed in 1964. 'How are they?'

'They're fine. Although sometimes I still get a little twinge – there's like a dot where the skin has healed round the nerve.'

'You want to get that looked at,' Patrick suggested.

We were filming with Bill Dysart and just before she became a huge star, Hannah Gordon, who was – and still is – a lovely, warm person.

The next day I wasn't required for filming so I went to Hammersmith Hospital and told them about my 1964 accident. I was sent to a finger specialist.

'Ah yes, I see what you've got,' he said. 'It's a pyogenic granuloma.'

'Oh. Is that life-threatening? Is it terminal?'

'No, it's just where the nerve-end comes to the surface and the skin heals round it. Come with me.'

I walked into his anteroom. The doctor laid a sheet of black velvet on the table. 'Put your hand on there with the finger outstretched and the other fingers back.'

I was beginning to worry. 'You're not going to cut my fingers open are you? You'll ruin that lovely piece of velvet.'

'Good lord, no.' He brought a little lamp out and set it up pointing at my hand. What kind of therapy was this?

'Doctor, will this hurt?'

'I shouldn't think so,' he said, producing a camera. 'I'm doing a book about hand injuries and I don't have a picture of a pyogenic granuloma. I'm going to photograph yours.'

So my finger did a photo shoot (for no fee!), and then the doctor took me back to the operating table and used a laser to burn the pyogenic granuloma off. I thought his book was more successful than his surgery, though; to this day I feel tingling if I happen to bang my finger hard.

We finished filming at Frensham Ponds with a scene where I said goodbye to the Doctor and his companions of the time, Polly and Ben, and the TARDIS dematerialised in front of me. Well, I say in front of me, of course that bit was done by camera trickery, but you know what I mean.

The next Monday we went to rehearsals in our little church hall just up from Shepherd's Bush and started working on the studio scenes. The way that most television was done back then was that all the location filming for a story was done first, and then the studio stuff was recorded later on – in this case resulting in my filming my leaving scenes before even having made the episodes!

The first episode was all taped in studio and when it was finished we were invited to see the result in Shaun Sutton's office. Everyone seemed pleased and so we moved onto record the rest of the episodes. Such was the pace that *Doctor Who* was made back then, that the first episode was recorded on the 3 December 1966, and then transmitted on the 17 December. A very fast turnaround.

I've always had a memory that after the first episode went out, the BBC began to get letters suggesting that it would be a good idea if Jamie stayed on as one of the Doctor's companions. Jamie had never seen electric light or motor-vehicles and he would be a touchstone for technological wonder. It was a neat parallel of the audience's apprehension of time travel and the four physical dimensions of the TARDIS.

However it seems that things are never quite as they seem. I do remember Innes taking me to one side.

'I say old boy, do you fancy staying on a bit longer? Maybe becoming part of the old TARDIS crew?'

'But how is that possible, Innes?' I asked. 'We filmed the ending with Jamie watching the TARDIS disappear.'

'Leave that to me.'

A few days later, we went back to Frensham Ponds and filmed a different ending in which this time Jamie said goodbye to his laird and to Hannah Gordon and got into the TARDIS.

Apparently it was my performance in those initial location scenes which convinced Innes to keep me on, and the additional filming there (which actually took place on the 21 December) was organised to provide me with my TARDIS entrance.

My agent hadn't told me that the BBC had actually taken an option on my services for three more adventures in the TARDIS. Secretly, Shaun Sutton had wanted the character of Jamie to take off, and it did. Which was lucky for me because I enjoyed three of the most wonderful years with Patrick Troughton and the team. However, as the script writers didn't know if Jamie was going to stay or not they hadn't written many lines for him in the first few adventures. My first story after 'The Highlanders' was 'The Underwater Menace', so I was paired off with Michael Craze, who played Ben the Cockney seaman, and shared his lines! Then in the next story 'The Moonbase' he (Jamie) was rendered unconscious in the first episode and ended up lying in a medical centre on the Moon pretty much until the next story! It was great for me – no lines to learn and a long kip on set!

Patrick Troughton was a lovely man and a brilliant actor. He was slightly eccentric. He wore the same pair of Hush Puppies for the entire three years, as Patrick, and as the Doctor. This was in rehearsal and on television. He was a very private man. He wouldn't talk about his exploits in the War. He never liked talking to the press. The most popular sixties TV chat show was *Dee Time* with Simon Dee and they pressed repeatedly for Patrick and I to go and make a live appearance. But Patrick would have none of it.

'I'm the Doctor,' he would say. 'What they see is me. When the credits roll at the end of the show I go back to being Patrick Troughton and that's it.'

One day Patrick and I were having lunch and I ran into Colin Douglas, one of my colleagues from the old Shaun Sutton repertory company from way back. I greeted him warmly and we began to reminisce but were interrupted by a dulcet female voice.

'Colin, I think we'd better go back to rehearsal now.'

I turned, and fell headlong into the loveliest pair of eyes I had seen for years. They belonged to a girl called Pamela Franklin.

Colin was doing a show called *Quick Before They Catch Us* and

Pamela was starring in the show with Teddy Green and David Griffin, long before David went on to become one of the stars of *Hi-Di-Hi*.

'Colin,' I said. 'Aren't you going to introduce me?'

'Oh yes, sorry. This is Pamela.'

I shook her hand. I wanted to hold it indefinitely.

'I loved you in *The Lion*,' I blurted out.

This was a film she made in Africa when she was ten.

'Thank you very much.'

'And I like *Quick Before They Catch Us* too,' I stammered.

'Why thank you. Come on, Colin, we must go back to work.'

I watched her go, already smitten. All I could think about that night was Pamela. I tossed and turned in bed unable to sleep. I considered ringing Colin the next day, or turning up to rehearsals, or maybe just bumping into them accidentally on purpose … But that seemed too corny.

Call Colin. That was the thing to do. Or at least it would be if I had happened to have his phone number.

One way or another I was quite determined that I should see that girl, and those eyes, again. And this time I would try not to stammer and drool like a teenager. I felt I had been gauche enough on our first meeting. I didn't want our second to be embarrassing. I decided to write her a letter. You know the sort of thing, 'Dear Pam … lovely to meet you the other day … I'm doing *Doctor Who* … I have the odd day off – do you …? Could we have lunch …? Give me a call …' That way if she found me too cheeky or if she just didn't fancy me, she could just bin the letter.

I counted one day for the letter to get to her. I was up with the larks the following morning in excited anticipation. I went downstairs looking for a letter in reply … nothing. Oh well.

Later that day the phone rang.

'May I speak to Frazer, please.'

'Speaking.'

'Hello, its Pamela. Thank you for the lovely letter.'

She had got it! She had responded! 'Hi, Pam, how are you?'

'I'm fine thanks. Look, I'd love to come to lunch. That sounds lovely. I live at Ashdown Forest in Sussex.'

'I'm in Chiswick. Perhaps I could meet your train.'

'I'd like that. Now the question is when. Would tomorrow be alright?'

My heart skipped a beat. I had the next day off so that was perfect. 'Wonderful.'

I couldn't wait till the next day to see her.

I met her off the train at Victoria and took her to see the film *Funeral in Berlin*. I spent the entire duration of the film wanting to put my arms around her, but thinking it might be too presumptuous. After the film we had an early supper and I walked her back to the station.

'I have enjoyed myself,' she said.

'Me too. Shall we do it again?'

'Why not?'

I kissed her on the cheek before she went. I caught one glimpse of those dazzling eyes as she waved goodbye over her shoulder and that was the start of seven or eight joyous months with Pamela. Every Saturday I would finish in the studio, get into my car and drive down to see her. I'd get there at about 10.30 and she would be waiting up for me with a kiss, a cuddle and a cup of cocoa.

Pamela's parents ran the post office at Ashdown Forest and her brother played cricket for the local village team. Pretty soon they roped me in too, and every Sunday for a season I played against the neighbouring villages like Coleman's Hatch and Uckfield.

We visited some friends of Pamela's down on the south coast and after supper, one lovely moonlit night, Pamela and I went for a walk along the sea front. There was a violent electrical storm over France and we stood staring out to sea watching it. I knew that I loved her and wanted to tell her so.

I turned to her and said, 'There's a storm raging over in France.'

'There's one in my heart too,' she said.

And we kissed and declared our love for each other.

We had so much fun together. I remember we went to a pop ball in

Wembley. I was mobbed. Oh yes, don't find it so amusing: there were days when Hines was mobbed by screaming teenagers. Clothes torn off – you name it. I was separated from Pamela by two security guards who rescued me and took me up to the VIP lounge. I pointed down to Pam, who was in the crowd.

'Can you fetch me that girl, please?'

'No, you want that one there,' said the guard pointing to a busty blonde.

'You don't understand; she's my girlfriend.' I again pointed to Pam.

'Of course she is,' he answered, winking at me. 'I'll fetch you the big blonde.'

At that moment a voice from the crowd rang out, 'Darling I can't get to you.'

''ere she called you darling.'

'Yes, she really is my girlfriend!'

Looking somewhat disappointed at not being able to rescue the big busty blonde, he said, 'I'll get her for you then.'

So he rescued Pam.

I was besotted with her and heartbroken when she got a part in a film directed by John Huston called *Sinful Davey*. It meant she had to go to Ireland.

'I'll ring you every day,' Pam promised and she kept her word.

Then one day I rang and said, 'I'm coming over next weekend …'

'Well … I'd rather you didn't. We're frightfully busy that weekend,' she said – and something in her voice told me that her reasons for not wanting me there we emotional rather than practical. It turned out that she had begun a relationship with the leading man, John Hurt.

Meanwhile, in *Doctor Who* we had a new female companion. Anneke Wills, who played Polly, and Michael Craze, playing Ben, had left in 1967, and joining us was Deborah Watling. Patrick and I were both thrilled. Here was a lovely young actress at the start of her career. We had both seen her in an episode of the BBC's *The Wednesday Play* called *Calf Love* with Simon Ward, and we thought she would be an asset in the TARDIS.

Deborah's first adventure with us was 'The Evil of the Daleks', set in Victorian London. As usual on *Doctor Who*, the first day on set was hilarious. We were filming at a very old house near Harrow which had belonged to W S Gilbert (of Gilbert and Sullivan fame). Deborah was playing a petite, staid Victorian girl wearing a crinoline. She had been kidnapped by the Daleks and held prisoner in this old house, and I had to run round looking for her. My first line to her was, 'Quick Miss Waterfield, up your passage-way.' This struck me at the time as wildly funny and I couldn't manage to say it with a straight face. On the occasions when I did get through the line, the crew would fall about laughing. We had to paraphrase the line for me before we could wrap the scene.

I was so looking forward to working with the Daleks – I wanted to ride in one. Now it is an unwritten rule that you don't touch the props in case you break them. I broke that rule. At lunchtime, when the set was deserted, I opened the lid of a Dalek, climbed in and started to scoot around the set. I was back to method acting – I was that Dalek. Suddenly I heard voices so I stopped. Two actors came on to the set and before I had chance to clamber out, they leaned on my Dalek and proceeded to tear the show to pieces: 'Bad scripts' … 'Director couldn't direct a pig to be dirty', etc, etc. After about five minutes of listening to this garbage I decided to take action. The Dalek spun into motion, moving away. In Dalek monotone I said, 'I-heard-that. I-heard-that. I'm-going-to-report-you.' As I moved they fell on the floor dumbfounded. Can you imagine, say, leaning on a wardrobe and suddenly it walks away? Oh the laughter when they realised I was inside, after some playful blackmail of course!

We had a scene where Patrick and I were looking for Debbie and we found a handkerchief. I had to say, 'Doctor, this is Miss Waterfield's. I'd recognise it anywhere.'

Well, I secretly switched the handkerchief for a pair of knickers. On our final rehearsal when we were looking for Deborah, I pulled out the knickers and said, 'Doctor, these are Miss Waterfield's. I'd recognise them anywhere!'

Off-camera, Deborah's voice rang out, 'They are not!'

Those knickers went from strength to strength. Marius Goring was playing an evil professor in the story. He was a marvellous actor to work with and also great fun. He borrowed the knickers and put them in his top pocket. In one scene when he was trying to put a positronic brain into one of the Daleks, (or as he teasingly said in every rehearsal, 'A suppositronic brain …') he said, 'My God! It's hot in here!' and whipped out the knickers to mop his brow.

A Dalek came into the scene with the knickers on the end of his plunger: 'Are-these-Miss-Wat-er-field's? Are-these-Miss-Wat-er-field's?'

The ethos on *Doctor Who* was that it was supposed to be fun. Patrick and I were both clowns and anybody who joined the cast tended to fall in with us so that there was a very playful spirit on the show. A lot of the practical jokes were adolescent, but that's often how high spirits express themselves.

A lot of silly jokes involved knickers as well, if we're being honest. There was the occasion when Jamie, the Doctor and a character called Isobel, played by Sally Faulkner, had to climb a rope ladder into a helicopter and it occurred to me that the rotors of a low-flying helicopter must create a huge down-draft that would hit the concrete and blow up again. My imagination conjured a vivid picture of Jamie's kilt blowing up to his shoulders, so I persuaded the director that being a gentleman, Jamie would let the lady go first. Sure enough, when Sally climbed the rope ladder her skirt blew up. After lunch it was my turn and there was considerable anticipation among the cast and crew: *what does Jamie wear beneath his kilt?* I had read somewhere that the Queen has little lead weights sewn into her skirts so that a sudden gust of wind doesn't reveal the royal thighs. My dresser was fishing at lunchtime, so I obtained some lead weights from him, and borrowed the crafty idea of Her Majesty, to the disappointment of the curious throng. Despite the helicopter and the blast of air, my kilt hung modestly down.

Doctor Who had always been fun, even my first story, 'The Highlanders'. One of the lines I had to deliver to the rest of the Highland prisoners in the hold of a galleon that was transporting us was, 'Look! A rat!' And there floating at our ankles was a stuffed rat. After a quick word with the wardrobe and props departments, on the next rehearsal I said the words, 'Look! A rat!' and the camera panned down to see said rat wearing a striped swimming costume and dark glasses.

Another of the great things about *Doctor Who* was all the friends I made, and among them was Nicholas Courtney, who had joined us to play Brigadier Lethbridge-Stewart. He actually appeared in a couple of stories, first as a Colonel, and then promoted to Brigadier. Now Nick is a lovely man and I'm so pleased to say that all these years later we are still good friends and when we attend *Doctor Who* conventions we always crack open a bottle of wine and reminisce. He fell in with us immediately. Like us, he enjoyed gambling on the horses, or playing cards or liar dice in the little anteroom. Often a director would come in with his hands on his hips to enquire whether we boys were coming to work today?

'I've got a good hand here,' Nick would say. 'We'll be there in a minute. Don't worry old boy, we've learnt the lines.'

Mind you, no matter how conscientious you are about learning lines, from time to time everybody dries. Nicholas was crafty about losing his lines. If Patrick forgot a line he would fluff and get round it. I would break out in a coughing fit and stop the take, asking for a glass of water. Nick's technique for covering was this: if he forgot his line he would look at the director and say, 'Duggie, am I meant to be standing here right now?' *Groan: Nick's forgotten his lines again …!*

Patrick and I had a great working relationship. We only had to look at each other to know how to plan the next gag or practical joke. It was almost like telepathy. We were filming on the coast at Margate one cold February in 1968. Patrick, Debbie and I had a scene where we were walking along and encountered this foam on the beach – it was actually the foam they used to put out fires on aircraft and the special effects department had laid us out a carpet of the stuff for filming. We only had one chance at doing it because when we walked into it would disturb the foam and it would disperse. I looked at Patrick and he looked at me and then we both looked at Deborah. Jamie and the Doctor decided on the spot to have some fun with Victoria.

We rolled Deborah in the foam and the cameras kept rolling.

'You swine! You swine!' cried Deborah, but she had to stay in character and we caught the whole thing on film.

By this time I was dating an actress called Susan George and she had come to watch the filming. There was a method in my madness. It had occurred to me that if ever Deborah wanted to leave the show it would be convenient if Suzy became the new companion.

On this particular day the TARDIS actually landed in the sea off Margate and we had to get into a rubber dingy to get to shore. We spent about two hours paddling around the sea while they got various shots. I was at the front kneeling down, in Jamie's kilt, and the sea water was lapping up the front of the dingy. My knees were getting colder and colder. Eventually my knees were blue with cold. I would never have believed it if I hadn't seen it with my own eyes. Susan grabbed a towel from the wardrobe department, fell to her knees and began massaging the life back into my knees. The looks on everybody's faces! Susan got the colour back into my knees and put her arms around me. A cameraman came up and said, 'Any chance of borrowing your kilt tomorrow, Frazer?'

My poor knees in that kilt! If you are ever asked to go horse-riding wearing a kilt, take my advice, say no. I only did it myself for the sake of art. I had to ride this marvellous stunt horse called Viking, gallop through the heather, throw myself out of the saddle and land on Peter Diamond, bringing him to the ground. (Peter was our stunt arranger on *Doctor Who*. I killed him so many times that he named his son Frazer after me.) After three or four takes my knees were red raw on the inside and all the hairs had been worn away. So all the way home I had a make-up girl rubbing liniment into my inside leg. Well, the kilt does have some advantages!

Doctor Who had many special effects, most of them functional, well they had to be, but if one went wrong it was always hilarious. Let me explain. When an Ice Warrior kills you, your body appears on screen to convulse in a heap. This is how they did it. The actor would hit a mark in front of a tall shiny mirrored piece of rubber. A prop man standing behind would pull a string and the camera would show the reflection of the actor's body convulsing and shivering, in and out. On one actual take an actor was being chased by an Ice Warrior: 'Die,' the creature hissed. He hit the mark, the prop man pulled, but the string came off the rubber mirror: no convulsing. The actor stood still, the Ice Warrior standing there, weapon raised, but to no avail. The Warrior's voice then sounded loud and clear: 'Shit. Missed the bugger!' The actor fell in a heap, not dead, laughing.

Soon it was time for Deborah to leave us. She wanted to move on to other things. We were very sorry to see her go. But, I thought, this was an opportunity to get Susan in. I suggested it, but her agent wanted her to go on to films, and in retrospect her agent wasn't a bad judge if you think of the brilliant movie career she's had.

Deborah left and the new girl was the lovely, elfin Wendy Padbury. She played a character called Zoe who took over after Debbie left in 1968. Wendy was sitting between Patrick and me in the rehearsal room in the old church hall one day, bent over her script in deep concentration. She was wearing a mini-kilt, a white blouse and little white boots. Patrick and I telepathically had the same idea – I undid her kilt on my side and Patrick undid her kilt on his side, and then we nudged her and said, 'Quick Wendy, it's our scene; we're on!' She leapt up and ran into the middle of the rehearsal room, and realised that her kilt was still sitting on the chair. She made a grab for it, but Patrick caught it up and threw it to me. Wendy was chasing us for her kilt when the vicar happened to walk in. Wendy, in her blouse, pants and boots, didn't miss a beat. She curtsied prettily. 'More tea Vicar?' she said.

One day, I got a phone call out of the blue. It was Pamela. She was back from filming *Sinful Davey* and wanted to take me to the premiere. I thought we were finished and I was ready to be cool with her but her directly asking me out like that took the wind out of my sails. I still carried a torch for her, so I said yes.

I escorted her to the premiere and we had supper afterwards. Even despite what had happened between us, the look was still in her eyes. Yes, I still wanted her. She intimated she would be keen to carry on where we left off. She wanted to have lunch the following day.

Well, I had a lunch date with Susan, so I did something foolish. I told Pamela that I couldn't see her because I had an audition that day. Susan and I had lunch and I rang Pamela that afternoon and suggested supper or a show the following night.

'How did the audition go?'

'Fine,' I lied.

'It was at the studios wasn't it?'

'Yes. It was.'

'And who did you lunch with?'

'The casting director.'

'Susan George has gone into casting then, has she?'

'Well,' I said slowly, 'I did see Susan for lunch as well ...'

'I think, Frazer,' said Pamela carefully, 'I'll bow out gracefully.'

I tried to talk her out of it, but she meant what she said. Shortly afterwards she went to America where she eventually married an American actor.

I was great friends at this time with Alan Whitehead, who was the drummer of the pop group Marmalade, who had a huge hit with 'Ob-La-Di, Ob-La-Da' at the start of 1969. We were Western riding freaks and whenever we had a weekend off Alan and I, and sometimes my brother Roy, would don our cowboy gear and get in the car and mosey on down to the Flying 'G' Cowboy Ranch in rattlesnake-infested Red Indian Hampshire. We'd play cowboys and Indians through the wonderful New Forest, stop for a sandwich and a glass of beer someplace, put the saddles back on, and hightail it back home. The Flying 'G' was great fun, but I regret to say now it has gone to that great prairie in the sky.

I know that because we turned up one day and it was shut. 'Never mind,' said Alan. 'I've got a couple of fans in Bournemouth: we'll go and see them instead!'

We checked into a hotel and the two girls came to our room. We went to town. Champagne, caviar, lobster, the lot! One massaged me on the bed whilst the other gave Alan a bath. Then we swapped. I had a bath and Alan got a massage. Midnight found us all in the swimming pool, doing all those things naked swimmers do! When we got back to London we felt guilty and decided to come clean to our girlfriends. We sat them down and I said, 'We have a confession to make – we met two girls in Bournemouth ...' Then I told them the whole story. They looked at us both for a second and then Sheila, Alan's girlfriend said, 'You boys, you live in your own little dream world. Bathing, massaging – in your dreams.' Do you know they didn't believe us! I tell you, always tell the truth and the bigger the story is, the less likely it is to be believed!

Knocking about with Alan as I did, I fancied my chances as a pop singer as well. So my brother Iain, now back from Germany, and a friend of his wrote a song for me in 1968 called 'Time Traveller'. We cut a demo disc, but nothing came of it. One of Iain's great pals was Alex Harvey (later of the Sensational Alex Harvey Band). He came up with another number called, 'Jamie's Awa' on the Time Machine'. We cut that, but still no record deal materialised.

I was playing football for the Showbiz Eleven. Barry Mason was down the left wing and radio DJ Diddy David Hamilton was down on the right. (Jess Conrad was in goal, which he preferred on the grounds that, 'Dear heart, I get to wear a different costume from you lot!')

Barry Mason and his partner Les Reed had just had a number one with 'Delilah' for Tom Jones, and they also wrote 'The Last Waltz' for Engelbert Humperdinck.

Barry and Les wrote me a song called 'Who's Doctor Who?' Major-Minor records agreed to put it out. We went to the studio and recorded the song for the A-Side, and 'Punch and Judy Man', written by Tommy Scott, for the B. Of the two I preferred 'Punch and Judy Man', but with the *Doctor Who* connection, 'Who's Doctor Who?' had to be the A-Side.

This is it, I thought. *I'm going to be a millionaire pop singer. Move over Tom Jones and Engelbert Humperdinck.*

The record was released, and at the same time Major-Minor had David

McWilliams singing 'Days Of Pearly Spencer' and Malcolm Roberts with 'May I Have The Next Dream With You?' The three of us would go out on one-night stands promoting our records and I used to love playing those one-nighters with the groupies screaming at me.

And in the end, David's record was a hit; Malcolm's was a hit. And mine was the only flop that Les Reed and Barry Mason ever wrote!

My father retired and with his pay-off and with my *Doctor Who* earnings the two of us bought a big house in Airedale Avenue, Chiswick. It had to be big, not only was Iain now back and living with us, but we had Mike Randle (my friend from Corona – remember the back seat of the MG?) and his brother, David lodging too! Dad wasn't a big man, he never raised his hand or his voice and we all saw him as a survivor. Roy was managing a bookmaker's shop called Hooper & Cox and Dad was working part-time for him. On the odd day off I would go and help him 'chalk the board' (put the runners and riders on the blackboard: no computer screens in those days). Everything in the Hines' household was rosy. Huh! Rosie, that name. It was Rosie, a neighbour's daughter, who brought me the fateful news one afternoon at the launderette.

'Frazer,' she almost screamed in her panic. 'Your father's ill, come home quickly.'

I left her with the washing and dashed back home to find my mother in the breakfast-kitchen. 'Quick Frazer: your father's had a heart attack.'

Dad was lying on the floor.

'What happened?'

'He was in the garden. He came in and said, "Here are some flowers for the woman I love." Then he just clutched his chest and collapsed.'

'What have you tried?'

'Nothing – I don't know what to do!'

I fell to my knees and held his nose trying to resuscitate him. His chest rose as I blew air into him. 'He's breathing!' I blew again. I didn't realise that I was blowing air into a dead man's lungs and it was just making his chest rise and fall. 'Call an ambulance!' I told my mother.

'I have done.'

I kept working at him, filling his lungs with air.

When the ambulance arrived I handed over to the ambulance men.

'Oh yeh,' said one. 'DOA.'

I knew what that mean. Dead On Arrival. 'He's not, he's not!' I cried. 'Use electric shock treatment, give him adrenaline, do something!'

I had seen enough hospital dramas to know the procedure. But this was the real world.

'We don't have those things with us.'

They picked up my father on a stretcher and put him in the back of the ambulance. My mother and I got in and went with them. We kept looking at Dad lying there very still, hoping that his chest would start to rise and fall on it own. But he was already gone. The doctors persuaded us that there was nothing more anyone could do. So, grief-stricken, we went home.

I felt as though I would never laugh again.

You just can't imagine anything ever being funny again. The one small comfort was that Iain, Roy, Mum and I were all in the house that night. The whole family mourned together.

I went to work the next day wearing a black armband. Patrick was the first to see me. He put his arms around me.

'Sorry to hear about your dad, old boy.'

After a few days I took the armband off. People kept asking me who it was for and whenever I tried to explain that my dad had died, my eyes would fill with tears. Eventually it caused me too much grief to keep talking about it.

I had the day off for my father's funeral. And then it was back to work. I was feeling very low. A friend of mine from the old recording days called Mike Wade called up to invite me to a party.

'Mike, I'm really not in a party mood right now.'

'It'll take you out of yourself.'

'I don't think so, Mike.'

'Well, look; I haven't got a car. Will you give me a lift at least?'

So I gave him a lift to Oakley Street in Chelsea. 'Now you're here,' he said, 'you might as well have one drink.'

'We rang the doorbell and were greeted by a vision of loveliness, Meredith Wilson. She looked at me with big sad eyes. It turned out that the reason for that sadness was that she had just lost her father as well. Whereas I had been press-ganged by Mike into going to the party, she had been press-ganged by her flatmate into giving it in the first place; we were in the same boat.

Neither of us was in a festive mood, so we went to her bedroom and sat on the floor talking about our fathers. At the end of the evening she slipped off a gold chain, with a gold Pekingese dog hanging from it, from around her neck and handed it to me.

'I'd like you to wear this always to remind you of the first evening we met.'

We kissed long and passionately and I was reluctant to leave. But we saw each other the next day and our relationship blossomed.

I had a few days off and I was planning to get away from it all. I asked her to come with me and she jumped at the chance to get away from London. So we hopped into my little white Brabham Viva and drove up to Fort William in Scotland. The next few days were bliss for me, walking around lochs hand in hand with one of the most beautiful girls I had ever seen and indulging in fine Scottish fare in the evenings.

I loved Meredith and I loved my white Brabham Viva but I didn't mind letting go of it when the time came. This is how it happened. I saw an advert in *Motorsport* for those little windscreen jets in the shape of the Mannequin Pis in Brussels, which is a statue of a little boy weeing into a fountain. You could get two tiny silver versions of the little boy to spray your windscreen. I thought this was funny and I mentioned it to Patrick. He didn't believe that there was such a thing.

'Honestly Patrick. You press a button on the dashboard and they wee all over your windscreen.'

'Get away with you!'

I wanted to prove it to him, but I had lost the magazine with the advert in it.

On my way home at some traffic lights in Richmond I stopped and noticed in a car showroom a white Rover 2000 with two Mannequin Pis's on the bonnet. I couldn't believe it. I pulled over and ran to look at this beautiful car. I asked the salesman the price of the Rover and how much he would give me for my Brabham. He was a bit perplexed, but looked it over. The Brabham Viva was a rare car and we made a deal. I wrote a cheque, rang my insurance company, and drove off in the white Rover 2000.

Is it just me, or was it easier to buy a car in those days?

The next day I took the car to rehearsals. I grabbed Patrick. 'Patrick, about this Mannequin Pis …'

'Oh don't start that again.'

'Honestly, there is such a thing. Look, I'll bet you ten quid. Ten quid says you can get windscreen washers in the shape of little boys that pee on your window.'

'All right Frazer, you're on.'

'Come with me.' I dragged him out of the building to the pavement and showed him the car. 'There you are.'

'My God! It's True! How did you find it?'

'I bought it on my way home last night.'

'It's your car? You little bugger! You don't mean to stand there and tell me that you bought a car just to get a tenner off me?'

'Anything, Patrick, to get a tenner off you!'

Along with the work and the cars was the other mainstay of 'celebrity' life, the charity appearances. One time, radio DJs Tony Blackburn and Ed Stewart, singer Sandie Shaw and many others including myself took part in a charity bike race to raise money for our then Olympic cycle team. The first prize was apparantly a pig (we thought it must be a side of bacon), second prize was a barrel of beer. We had to ride two laps of the track. Tony Blackburn set off like a scalded cat – we all chased him. On the last lap his chain broke and I was left in the lead. I won, stopped peddling the bike and promptly fell off – damn fixed wheels! Unfit and with legs of jelly I staggered to the toilets where I promptly threw up! In the next stall doing the same thing was Ed Stewart. When you've expended so much energy with little prior training it's almost inevitable you'll be praying to the china God in the gents! Revived, I went and picked up my prize – a wooden box, which to my amazement was moving and oinking! It was a live baby porker.

'Take it 'ome and have some nice suckling pig, lad,' someone said.

I took one look and thought no way. I took him home to Mum.

'Mum. We've got a new arrival.'

The piglet was so sweet and luckily Mum agreed we could keep him. We called him 'Whoey' after *Doctor Who* of course, and he lived with us in Chiswick. Clip-clopping on his little high heels, he would enter our kitchen from the garden, covered in mud. My mother would often shout, 'Get out of here, you filthy little pig!' and off he'd trot only to return about five minutes later clean as a whistle. Inevitably he grew too big and I offered him to Regent's Park for their Children's Corner but they replied that they could always feed him to the lions! So I took him on life's next adventure to live in Chessington Zoo in Kiddies Corner as 'Whoey, the *Doctor Who* Pig'.

One day I got a phone call, 'Whoey is too big to even walk now. We'll have to put him down. Do you want some of him?'

'What? To eat?' I cried horrified.

I didn't have the heart for that, well could you?

By now my agent was agitating for me to leave *Doctor Who*; she said I had done enough television and should now go on to films. Patrick Troughton was hearing the same thing from his wife. But we were enjoying ourselves. Every day it was a joy to come to work. We even had Pauline Collins on the show. We tried to persuade her to join us in the TARDIS and roam with us across space and time. But she declined, offering the opinion that her career was going elsewhere. We looked at her as she left – Pauline Collins. What a waste. To think she could have been with us in the TARDIS; and after all, what has she done since *Doctor Who*? Only won an Oscar!

I mentioned to my mother the possibility of leaving. She went ape.

She called Hazel and dressed her down.

'How dare you suggest that Frazer leave *Doctor Who*? He's the breadwinner now. He's the only man bringing money into the house. You can't expect him to leave.

'Darling, it's his *career*, and he ought to leave now.'

My mother and Hazel had the most awful row about it, but in the end I listened to my agent. With heavy heart I decided to leave the show.

'Hang on,' said Patrick. 'My contract finishes three months from now. Don't leave just yet; stay on for another three months. We'll finish together.'

We agreed to that and Wendy Padbury decided she didn't want to stay on with a new Doctor, so she would leave then as well.

Our last adventure was called 'The War Games', and was a ten-part story. We filmed it down at Brighton rubbish tip where previously they had been shooting *Oh What a Lovely War*. One scene required Patrick and me to be surprised by an explosion and we would realise we were in the middle of a First World War barrage. Patrick wanted to know how big the explosion was going to be, but the whole thing had been set up and our director wanted to get on and shoot it. But Patrick insisted, so to reassure him the explosives expert was called over to explain that there was nothing to worry about. When the fellow came over, half his face and several of his fingers were missing. He'd had an accident with an explosion for a Charlie Drake show a few months earlier. That made Patrick's mind up for him.

'Set the explosion off now. I want to see it before we go anywhere near it.'

The charge was duly set. There was a huge explosion and a big rock landed just on the spot where Patrick was supposed to be standing.

'Yes,' said Patrick in that dry, understated way of his. 'I'm glad we had this little test.'

It was in the last few days of shooting *Doctor Who* that I came across a slim, long-haired blonde girl in the corridor. When she turned around I thought, *I recognise that face!*

'Liza!' I called. 'Liza Goddard!'

I hadn't seen her since we were children, back when I was nine or ten years old. Liza and I used to play together. Now, a dozen years on, here she was looking tall and beautiful.

'Where've you been?'

'Australia,' she said.

'Oh that's right! You were in *Skippy*. What are you doing now?'

'I'm starting a new show called *Take Three Girls*. I think it's going to be rather good.'

'It's great to see you,' I said, and it was.

On my last day of shooting *Doctor Who*, Liza and I went for a coffee to catch up, talking about all the old times. For some reason, it didn't occur to us that there would be new times to take their place.

Chapter Five
I Hang Up My Kilt

Rusty, Meredith's mother, had a villa over in Ibiza, so after I had finished *Doctor Who*, off we flew with her to while away the summer, lying by the villa pool during the day and eating long languorous dinners by night. It was balmy and good and we were very happy. We bought a little Volkswagen microbus, a run-down little rust-bucket, to get around the island. We called it our 'hippy-happy home on wheels'. It had only two seats at the front and we would stick old deck-chairs in the back and pile off to the beach. It felt like the summer would last forever and we didn't mind if it did.

The idyll was interrupted by a call from my agent who wanted me to return to England to audition for a film. I flew back home and met the director, James Clavell, a very tall gentleman. After he merely talked to me for a while I was dismissed. He had seen all he needed to, so I went back to Ibiza. Ten days later, Hazel phoned again. I had the part. I was to play a character called Corg in a film called *The Last Valley*, starring Michael Caine and Omar Sharif. They were already in Austria where filming had begun.

I was elated, although sorry to leave Meredith and Rusty in Ibiza. My idea was that I would fly back home and prepare for the film and Meredith could join me the next week. This sounded good to her.

I flew back to London and underwent my medical check. Everybody has to be cleared by sawbones for insurance purposes before starting a big film. I rang Meredith to notify her that I was due to fly on Monday and that, for us, the lotus-eating was over. 'When are you coming back?'

'Well,' she said, 'the weather really is wonderful over here.'

I knew that. It had been glorious all the time I was there. 'All good things come to an end, darling. I'd like to see you before I go to Austria.'

'I'll see,' she said.

I thought this was an odd response. What was there to see? Meredith didn't work, and she was not restricted in her holidays like most people.

She could always go back to Ibiza after she'd seen me. The next day she called me again. I was becoming frustrated.

'Darling, when are you coming back?'

'We're waiting for my brother, Mark, to come and join us for a few days holiday. He'll be out soon.'

'And you'll see him and come straight home? Because you know I'm off to Austria in just a couple of days.'

'Yes, I'll … see him.'

The next day I rang her with some good news. I wasn't going to Austria quite yet. The film was behind schedule and I had an extra week in London: she could still see Mark, and come and spend a few days with me in Chelsea before I went. She said that would be OK.

But four days later I still hadn't see hide nor hair of her. I called again. Mark was there. They were having a lovely time. Great: so was she coming home? No. She wanted to stay a little longer with her brother. I suggested that she come home now, and she could go back to Ibiza as I flew out to Austria. But she was settled. She wanted to stay in Ibiza.

'Meredith, I want to see you before I go. I'll be gone for two, maybe three months.'

'That's OK. I'll see you when you get back.'

'I didn't understand her attitude, 'No, I want to see you now. Look, if you're not on the next plane, you can forget it.'

'Oh, don't be like that. You know how good the sun is here.'

'I don't care. It might be freezing in England, but if you love somebody you want to be with them.'

'I'll think about it.'

She wasn't on the next plane, or the one after that! When we next spoke she suggested that if I rang her from Austria, she'd catch up with me there. I said that might be difficult, I would be working. I didn't know what my accommodation would be. Fine, she said. Then she would stay in Ibiza.

I was somewhat down about all this as you can imagine, but fate had a funny way of intervening.

That evening the phone rang. It was Liza. 'Hello, I've got tickets to a premiere. Do you want to escort me?'

'I would be delighted to.'

Recently I found a photograph of Liza and I at that premiere. I was wearing a pink monogrammed, Chinese-style dinner jacket; she was a little more discreet in a long black velvet cloak. Seeing those clothes, it all came flooding back, the evening out, the times I spent with Liza, everything. We enjoyed the premiere and supper afterwards, and the next day I thought I'd show off by taking her for a lunch of oysters and Chablis. I'd turned on to oysters years previously in 1966 when I'd been working with Bernard Lee on a series called *King of the River*. I was playing a fisherman called Bob Elliot in a lifeboat crew down at Whitstable and Bernard was our skipper, Joss King.

'Ever had oysters?' Bernard asked when we had finished filming one day. I hadn't. 'Right, oysters for lunch!'

So we went to an oyster bar.

'Bernard, aren't you supposed to tip them into your mouth and swallow them whole?' I asked.

'No, chew the bastards!'

I had the feeling over lunch with Liza that there was just a little spark of electricity. I didn't want it to end; I didn't want to let her go. We went out that night as well and we met for lunch again the following day. Within the space of eight days I had given up calling Meredith. After all, she clearly no longer wanted to see me.

By this time, *The Last Valley*, like so many pictures shot on location, was well behind schedule on account of the weather. My departure for Austria was repeatedly delayed. Eventually I received a phone call which notified me that I was now needed and that a courier was on his way with a first-class ticket to leave the following morning. Naturally I made arrangements to see Liza for supper that night.

About five o'clock, while I was getting ready to go and pick Liza up, the phone rang. It was Meredith.

'Hello, darling. I'm home.'

'Home?'

'Back from Ibiza. And in time for dinner, so where are you taking me?

'Meredith, I asked you weeks ago to come back. I've got plans for supper tonight.'

'Who with?'

'It's none of your business.'

'And tomorrow?'

'Tomorrow I'm going to Austria,' I told her.

'I see. Well, can we meet before that?'

'I don't think there's any point. Your holiday was obviously more important to you than spending the time with me, so that's it.' And it was.

The next day I flew out to Austria with another actor guy called Mark Edwards. As we were the new boys on the film we quickly struck up a friendship on the flight over.

We arrived at our hotel, the Maria Theresia in Innsbruck. This hotel was apparently named after Princess Maria Theresia who was afflicted with an unfortunate deformity. She had no breasts at the front, but a perfect pair on her back. By all accounts she was very ugly, but fun to dance with! My room was splendid and I thought, *I'm going to like it here!*

Mark and I went down to supper together and the first assistant director, Bill Cartlidge, came over. He introduced himself and asked us if we'd like to meet Michael Caine. We were introduced and I found Michael very affable and agreeable. In ten minutes we had settled into an easy relationship and we all spent the entire evening telling each other jokes. We were both great Tommy Cooper fans and spent so much time 'doing' Tommy Cooper that by the end of the film even Omar Sharif was going, 'Jus' like that!'

I was having a great time, although missing Liza very much. I looked forward to her long letters which came every other day. I had brought with me a little portable record-player and a few of my favourite records. Whenever I was homesick for England and Liza I would play the Rolling Stones' 'Lady Jane'. I would sit in the dark and think of Liza sitting on the end of my bed and imagine running my fingers through her beautiful long blonde hair.

The Last Valley was set during the Thirty Years' War. James Clavell had built an entire old Austrian village up in the hills. When the filming wrapped they struck the set and were left with a large number of chickens and pigs that the props department had obtained. The animals had all bred, and I think they actually made a profit selling on the livestock to the local farmers at the end of the film.

All the actors had grown beards and long hair, and our costumes were the kind of thing in which I felt very comfortable – all cloaks and thigh boots and swords.

Two of the biggest horses on the film were a couple of enormous shire-type beasts called Windsor and Richmond. I was the smallest actor and also the new boy, so naturally they gave me the tallest horse to ride. Richmond was a great strapping grey, lovely to ride and very comfortable in those wonderful old padded saddles. I enjoyed riding him around the set when I wasn't working, but it was difficult for me to get on to this huge horse, so I swapped him for a smaller one called Waltz for the actual filming.

Now, the first scene I had to shoot called for me to ride up with a few other actors and stuntmen, we rein in, and fire our flint-lock pistols. We rehearsed this scene all morning, and then broke for lunch. Unknown to me one of the stuntmen, who was due to use Waltz later on, had grabbed the horse and put a falling bit on him. This is a special kind of bit which will cause the horse to fall to the ground when you rein him in.

After lunch we came back to shoot the scene. I leapt up onto Waltz. We rode up to the camera, I reined him in and Waltz thought, *I know this one* and promptly threw himself to the ground.

'Frazer, stop messing about,' James Clavell said.

'James, I'm not,' I replied in a muffled voice on account of being underneath the horse. Fortunately I had got my leg out of the way.

I had the odd line in the film, like 'Charge!', 'Get back!' and 'Have at thee!' but I also had a big scene with Michael Caine. I was really looking forward to it. I'd learnt my lines until I knew them backwards as well as working very hard on my accent.

The day came. I was in a band of cut-throats and vagabonds who attacked Michael's group. I was captured and thrown to my knees and had to beg Michael for mercy.

When the footage was in the can I was very satisfied with my scene with one of the stars of the film. I felt I had made my mark. There is a special satisfaction in a job well done. Now, if you ever go to Pinewood Studios, do have a look on the cutting room floor. My scene with Michael Caine may still be there. Or it may be in a dustbin. The one place it definitely isn't is in the final cut of the film!

By now I had struck up a friendship with Chris Chittell and if that name rings a bell it's because he went on to play the dastardly Eric Pollard in *Emmerdale*. In those days Chris was a long blond-haired, bearded, callow youth.

Boys on tour, or on holiday, or indeed, on location for films, get into all manner of scrapes. One night Chris had taken an Austrian girl back to his room to discuss the 'problems with Uganda!' Mark Edwards and I knew about this so we snuck out of our rooms and shifted a huge wardrobe in front of Chris' door. At two in the morning there was a muffled 'goodnight' and we heard, 'bonk': not the dulcet coupling of Chris and the Austrian girl, but the sound of his head hitting the wood as he tried to open his door outwards.

'Hines! Edwards!' I heard him call. 'Was this you? You bastards!!!'

We let him stew for a few minutes, during which his language became more and more colourful and our laughter got more and more helpless. Eventually we moved the wardrobe away and there was Chittell red-faced and spitting fire!

In the morning we were all friends again and we all spent breakfast quietly trying to think of good jokes to play on each other. But it was a very friendly film. In fact, almost everybody I have ever worked with has been good to know. Perhaps 99 per cent of them have been a joy, but of course, the ones who are vile and make the most noise get the most attention.

I played chess a couple of times with Omar Sharif. I beat him the first time – go on, be impressed! After that he started paying attention and thrashed me from then on. I happened to remark that I was going out with one of girls on the set that night.

'Do it in style,' Omar said. 'Take my car.'

And so he leant me his black Rolls Royce, complete with chauffeur, an inscrutable man named Tug, and we had a lovely elegant time. On the way home Tug pulled into a layby and I asked, 'Have we broken down?'

'No,' replied Tug, lighting a cigarette, 'Mr Sharif suggested I stop so you can say goodbye to the lady properly.' Then he walked away.

By the time he returned I was reading *War and Peace* and she was knitting a sweater. Lord knows what Omar used to get up to!

In the morning Omar wanted to know how it had gone.

'It was wonderful, Omar, thank you for the car.'

'The young lady … what was she like?'

'She was charming.'

'Do you mind if I take her out tonight?'

I didn't mind at all. I was only being friendly. My real girlfriend was back in England.

So he did take her out, in the same car, that very night; and I think that might be the only time on any movie set that anybody has taken a girl out *before* Omar Sharif.

In television if you have to drink wine in a scene it's normally Ribena. Well they don't have Ribena in Austria, or if they do, they don't substitute it for the real thing. On *The Last Valley* there were several huge barrels of red wine to which we had recourse when we were supposed to be drinking. There was a big wedding scene, and we were all dancing around and whooping it up. After a few visits to the wine barrels not a lot of acting was going on. By half past six in the evening we were due for a wrap, Mark Edwards, Chris Chittell and I, along with several others (including James Clavell's thirteen-year-old daughter, Holly!) were moderately ratted, lying on that Austrian hillside. And can I just say that if anybody is considering casting me in a movie in Austria, in summer, that has a drinking scene in it, please call my agent right now.

Once the location work finished we all packed our bags and boarded a coach for the airport. The English shooting was going to be done in my old stamping grounds of Frensham Ponds, where years earlier little Jan in *The Silver Sword* had helped Melvyn Hayes, Ingrid Sylvester and Pat Pleasence to escape from the Germans to Switzerland.

The film company had built the front of a castle with a huge drawbridge in the middle of a lake. We had a lot of night shoots to do where we would start at 6.30 pm and finish at six in the morning, and then, bleary eyed, get in our cars and drive home.

Liza came down one evening to see me filming. She had ridden over on Madrigal, a horse from Mrs Carters' riding school at Frensham Ponds. On her way, she told me, she paused to light a cigarette and when she tried to spur Madrigal on he wouldn't move.

'Come on Madrigal, don't be silly.'

But he wouldn't go on. She looked up. There in front of them along the lane was a row of gibbets with corpses hanging from them. They weren't real, of course – the prop men had mocked them up – but they gave her quite a turn. And Madrigal wouldn't go anywhere near them. So she had to find another way round.

Michael Caine is a really down-to-earth man with a great sense of humour. In the big battle scene he had to lead his band in an assault on the castle. Bob Porter, our associate producer, explained the scene to us: 'Michael leads you – his band – over the drawbridge, giving it a bit of roast beef and two veg,' (Bob's way of describing a sword fight) 'and you storm the castle.' Well, we stormed the castle in our manly fashion, giving it 'roast beef and two veg' and added a bit of salt and pepper as well. A cannon was brought up to the gates and blasted them open.

Michael strode through and raised his sword. 'That'll teach you not to invite us to your bleedin' party Clavell!'

James just had time to shout 'Cut!' before the desperate snarling army

My alter ego Joe Sugden in *Emmerdale Farm*.

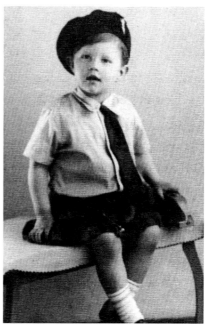

Left: My grandmother 'Mamma Scotland'. Right: Little Frazer … already preparing for the role as the Highlander Jamie in *Doctor Who*.

In Hamburg 1965 with the League of Gentlemen pop group in the room once occupied by the Beatles. I'm the unhappy looking one third from the left, top row.

Goodness those trousers itch! Me as Maurice Chevalier.

Top: That was some sneeze! Me (centre) with Ingrid Sylvester and Melvyn Hayes in *The Silver Sword*. (1957) Bottom: As Kim in a Children's Film Foundation production called *Peril for the Guy*. (1956)

Top: 'How much do we get per episode?' John Phillips as Elzevir Block and me as John Trenchard in *Smuggler's Bay*. (1964) Bottom: 'You too will be put on the list …' Playing a Radio Operator in *Zeppelin*. (1971)

'Has anyone seen my chickens?' As Corg in *The Last Valley*. (1970)

It's no wonder I was a jockey with a waistline like that!

Look at the legs on that! Me as an apprentice jockey. (1978)

dissolved into an anarchic crowd, helpless with mirth. The humour of the man at four o'clock in the morning!

There were a bunch of us with just odd lines in the film, none with very big parts. So any scenes one was in, one wanted to be in as much as possible. I think Chris Chittell must have stitched his costume to Michael's, because wherever Michael was, there was Chittell sharing a close-up or two-shot. I decided to confound him. The scene in question involved us riding up to the top of a hill on horseback. When we got to the top we would all jostle for a position to be next to Michael. This time Chittell seemed to have glued his horse to Michael's. So after the rehearsals, when we were all having our flintlock pistols loaded and Chris was leaning over his horse, I undid his girth. These were heavy old-fashioned saddles, not like the ones we use today. If the girth was undone the saddle wouldn't immediately fall off. With the weight right they would stay put for a while.

'First positions!'

We got ready to film the scene.

We trotted up the hill, spurs jingling, horses champing on the bits. Michael reined his horse in. Chittell eased his horse in near Michael to try to be in the shot. Suddenly he could feel something wrong. He was gently sliding. He tried to alter his weight. He was sliding more and more towards Michael, which was usually his intention, but this time was inadvertent. He tried to compensate by standing on his left stirrup, but it was no good and the saddle slipped to the ground with Chris in it.

'Cut! Chittell – stop messing around!'

It was only years later that I told Chittell the truth. It's a funny business, acting. You might be best friends with somebody on a film and then not see them for ten years.

I didn't see Chris again until he joined *Emmerdale* for six episodes twenty years after *The Last Valley*. He was in a bar telling the story of falling off his horse next to Michael Caine and turned to me to back him up.

'Chris, I have to own up,' I said. 'I was the man who undid your girth.'

'You bastard! I always thought it was Mark Edwards.'

Our final night on the film was a post-battle scene. We were all covered in blood and mud and we were variously afflicted with mock wounds. There were a couple of stuntmen with stumps attached to their tunics so that they looked as though they had lost limbs. The make-up department had done a real number on us. We were a sorry-looking rabble.

'Take your horses back to the stables,' said Bill Cartlidge, when the scene was in the can.

We were all tired and we set off to walk the horses back to the bivouacs on Frensham Ponds. The mist was swirling up over the Ponds, will-o'-the-wisp were dancing over the marshes and in that early morning the only sound was the clatter and creak of our armour and the saddles. The horses were sweating and steaming, heads down, and we made our weary way unspeaking, each one of us thinking forward to his bath and his bed.

Round the corner came a workman in a donkey jacket with a flat cap and wellington boots, swinging his bag of snap as he came. He stopped dead and his eyes grew wide. He stepped aside out of our way and as we passed him I looked at Chittell.

'What a battle that was, comrade,' I said.

The workman clutched his chest and staggered back into the bushes and we carried on like the spectral progress he obviously thought we were. For all I know to this day there might still be in that bush a skeleton in an old faded donkey jacket and wellington boots, bleached by the sun, his skeletal hand clutched to his heart. We don't know. We could have killed him.

We all went to see the premiere of *The Last Valley*. Michael Caine gave one of the finest performances of his career … and the film flopped. To this day it remains a mystery why.

It also remains a mystery why Liza and I split up. She just announced one day that we should go our separate ways. I don't think she enjoyed the Sunday jaunts to various venues to watch me play for the Showbiz XI. I think she had better things to do than stand on a windy touchline. *C'est la vie.*

At least my film career was looking up. Well, that's the way it seemed to me. I auditioned for a part in a film called *Zeppelin*, starring Elke Sommer and Michael York. I was up for the role of the radio operator on the zeppelin. You might have seen the film – it seems to be on television every bank holiday Monday – but in case you think I must be making a fortune from this exposure, I regret to tell you that one doesn't get repeat fees for films.

I met Michael, Elke and Marius Goring, who was playing a mad German professor called Professor Altschul. He always seemed to play mad professors – he had played one for us in *Doctor Who*.

I am always nervous on a first day – especially coming into a film that has been shooting for three or four weeks already – but my first scene went without a hitch. By the end of my first week I was well settled in and enjoying myself. As usual in the summer I was due to play cricket at the weekend. I love my cricket and most Sundays in the season will find me on a cricket pitch somewhere in England. This game was at Blenheim Palace and I was facing some nice slow bowling. The bowler knew I was in the middle of a picture and mustn't break any bones so he was playing a safe game. But I leaned forward for one ball and it hit the top of my bat, ricocheted up and hit me in the eye. I thought nothing of it and threw the ball back to the bowler. I took my guard and suddenly felt a little woozy. There was something running into my eye. I put my glove up to it: blood. They carried me off the pitch and my eye started to close. They took me into the beer tent and placed a tea towel full of ice over my eye. That helped a little but by the time I got home that day my eye was completely closed. It looked like I had gone fifteen rounds with Henry Cooper.

I had been here before. Like the morning back in 1964 when my fingers were stitched up. I had to drive to the film studio expecting the wrath of the director to descend on me like Jehovah in a strop. I walked into the make-up department at six o'clock in the morning.

'Can you do anything about this?' I asked.

'My God, what have you done? There's no way we can fix that! We'll have to go and see Etienne. Etienne Périer was the director.

'I'm sorry, Etienne. I was playing cricket yesterday and I kept my eye too closely on the ball.'

'*Merde,*' he said. 'What are we going to do about Frazer's eye?'

The set for the scene we were to shoot was my radio room. Michael York would come in and tell me that I was wanted down below and while I was gone he would break into my radio and send a message. Then I would come back, knowing that he had lied to me and discover my radio broken. He and I would have a big fight and he would knock me out. Fortunately we hadn't yet shot the scene where Michael was sending his message to England, so it was decided to shoot the bits immediately for which I was not required.

Over the next two or three days the swelling around my eye went down, leaving me with just the bruising. Etienne hit upon the idea of shooting the last past of the sequence first and taking advantage of my disfigurement. My bruising would be the result of the fight with Michael.

I got on very well with Michael and we worked out our fight scene together without the intervention of the stuntmen. It ended up with Michael reaching up and grabbing a fire-extinguisher, clocking me on the head with it and killing me. It was a pity I had to be killed because weeks later the rest of the crew went off on location to Malta. That trip would have been something to live for!

All that was left for me was a scene where I was dead and Michael threw me off the zeppelin into the sea. Marius Goring and I were standing down during a night shoot waiting for Etienne to get to us when Marius said, 'Frazer, I've got rather a nice bottle of claret in my dressing room; do you fancy a drop?'

Well I had no dialogue. I was dead. So I said that would be lovely. Even if Etienne needed me, a glass of wine wouldn't hurt.

'After we had done that claret justice, Marius said, 'I've got another bottle.'

About one o'clock we addressed ourselves to that one and showed it as much respect as we had the first. When we had finished it I remembered that I had a couple of bottles of claret in the boot of my car. We ended up accounting for four bottles of claret.

'Are you sure you have no dialogue, Frazer?'

'Oh yes; I'm dead.'

The second assistant director came to tell us that they weren't going to get to us that night and we could stand down. Good. We repaired to our respective dressing rooms and crashed out.

In the morning I was a little worse for wear. But, I reasoned, being dead shouldn't be too taxing. I lay in the chair and Michael York had to pick me up. Well, I'm heavy. Michael couldn't have treated me with delicacy, even if he had wanted to. His only option was to throw me over his shoulder, which gave me an intimation of just how ill I could conceivably be. *Careful Michael*, I thought. *Neither of us wants me to throw up all over you!*

He was to throw me over the side of the zeppelin. This meant a fall of ten or twelve feet on to a pile of cardboard boxes which the stuntmen had arranged for me. I hurtled down with my eyes closed, which is a rather strange feeling, even when it is a short fall. I landed in a heap, my head thumping, and I was deeply grateful that is was all over.

'Cut!' said Etienne.

'I think I'd like to do that one more time,' called the cameraman.

Oh no. The stuntmen set up the cardboard boxes again, and we went through the scene *four times!* Remind me never to be dead with a hangover.

Zeppelin finished and I bade my farewells to Michael, Elke, Etienne and the rest of the crew and then I went home to wait for my next film part to materialise … I'm still waiting.

It was back to treading the boards again.

In those days Bill Kenwright was a young producer struggling to make ends meet, trying his hand at putting on the odd show. He was being terribly ambitious with a musical called *No Trams to Lime Street*. It was based on the play by Alun Owen about three sailors who come back from their cargo ship in Liverpool. Ray Fell and Bill were in it and I auditioned for the part of Taffy. I sang, 'I've Grown Accustomed To Her Face' with a Welsh accent and Bill liked me, although he said he was trying to get Adam Faith for the part.

I went home terribly disappointed. I had really wanted the part and had worked hard on getting my Welsh accent right. But a week later Bill called me with the news that Adam Faith didn't want to play the role and I was in the running again. But could I just come and read for the director, Maurice Stuart.

'Get some more Welsh in to you, Frazer,' Bill said. 'I'd like you to play this part but I need you to be more Welsh.'

So I went to the record library and borrowed the Richard Burton version of *Under Milk Wood*.

The next day I went along to read for Maurice Stuart. I said in my best Richard Burton voice, 'Hello, my name is Taffy.'

Afterwards Maurice said, 'Yes, that's fine Frazer, although could you play it a little bit more like Taffy Owen and less like Richard Burton?'

I said I could and I got the part.

It was great fun. The set was very ambitious. It was rather like a conveyor belt bringing the sets on. We rehearsed and came to the technical run-through, which got so far behind that on the opening night when the curtain should have gone up at 7.30, we were still behind the safety curtain finishing the third-act run-through. By quarter to eight the audience was getting distinctly restless. By ten to eight they had started slow hand-clapping. I looked into the wings to an imaginary chauffer: 'Start the car!' I hissed.

Eventually we finished the run-through at five past eight. The overture started. We were up and running.

The curtain opened and we began our opening number. Edward Evans, that fine old actor, singing his heart out. I came on in my dungarees, playing third engineer and sang for all I was worth. We all gave it 110 per cent and we brought the audience round. Once we got going the audience were with us all the way … but we managed to shake them off at Kew Gardens!

Seriously, we finished to a standing ovation. The conveyor belt system scenery had continued to play up, bringing sets on and off half-way through scenes, The girl would be singing in the bar and the conveyor would start up on its own and slowly take her off stage in the middle of her song. These things happen in theatre and you have to rise above them.

There is a famous story of the opera singer Gerard Heinz who was singing the end of act one in *Lohengrin*. In his last few bars a huge mechanical swan came on stage and at the end of his song he would step on it and be carried off stage. Applause. Curtain. End of act one. One night the swan came on early in the middle of the song and Heinz watched it glide on and offstage out of the corner of his eye. He sang bravely on and when he came to the end of his aria he looked into the wings and asked, 'What time is the next swan?'

I had slightly gone off women at this time. There had been one or two troubled relationships and I had put my love life on 'hold'.

One of the dancers in the tour was a girl called Irene Gorst. After the show one night in Liverpool Irene asked if she could come back with me to my hotel for a drink. I didn't mind, so off we went. I bought her a drink in the bar and we had a sandwich and then she insisted on buying me a large brandy. We sat there talking in the bar until about half past one in the morning. At which point she gave me a funny look. She got up and came and sat on my lap and kissed me. I kissed her back. Well, I hadn't been looking for a relationship but the girl had been coming on to me and it seemed churlish to disappoint her. I asked her to my room.

'No, that's enough,' she said.

'What do you mean, that's enough?'

'It was a test.'

'I'm sorry; I don't follow you.'

'Well you haven't hit on any of the girls in the show. If you're a dancer you usually get chatted up sometime on the first rehearsal. There's always somebody trying to get into your knickers. But you've left us all well alone. Me and the rest of the girls were wondering if you were gay and I drew the short straw to find out. I had to kiss you to see whether you responded.'

I laughed. 'Did I pass?'

'My report to the girls will be that you're anything but!' she said with a twinkling smile. And with that she turned and left and I heard her high heels clicking out into the street.

Now, I'm not remotely homophobic – you'd better not be if you work in the theatre. But me? Gay? How could anybody think it? I thought about all my previous girlfriends and how they would respond to the suggestion. As I went up to my bedroom I thought I could hear the ghostly echo of their incredulous laughter.

We were all hoping that *No Trams* would come into the West End and be a huge success and we'd all make fortunes. But it didn't. If a show is going to fold, two weeks beforehand the company manager 'posts a notice' saying that 'with deep regret such and such a day will be our last performance …' Our notice was posted.

On the Friday before the last show, Bill called me into his dressing room.

'Frazer,' he said. 'I've lost a fortune on this show, I don't have the money to pay the wages. I can just about pay the dancers. Now look, your name is above the title on the posters. Could you possibly forgo your wages.

Actually I was only on £40 a week. In 1971 that wasn't bad money, but it wasn't exactly riches.

'Bill I've no work lined up for after this.'

Bill was wringing his hands. (I was ringing my agent!)

'All right, Bill,' I said thinking I was probably giving in too easily.

'I'll make it up to you,' he said. 'I'll give you more work, a West End play, whatever.'

'OK Bill. I'll hold you to that.'

'I won't forget this Frazer.'

Today, Bill Kenwright is a multi-millionaire producer of nine or ten West End shows at a time and I'm truly pleased for him. I hope he's reading this book, though, because, Bill, you still owe me a starring part in the West End!

But he did give me another part. The following year I toured with him in *Doctor in the House*. That was also a tour of mixed success. The bill poster read:

Tonight at the Adeline Genee Theatre, East Grinstead – six young TV stars: Bill Kenwright, Nigel Humphries (*Coronation St*), Frazer Hines (Jamie in *Doctor Who*), Johnny Wade (Stanley Millett in *Compact*), Carolyn Lister (*Crossroads*) and Patricia Fuller (*Coronation St*), in *Doctor in the House!*

We played that theatre, we six young TV stars, and on the Wednesday matinee the company manager said, 'I think you ought to know. Only one man had booked for this matinee.'

'Just one?'

'Just one.'

'On his own?'

'On his own.'

'So we scrub it, right?'

'You have to go on.'

'We can't do the show for one bloke in the stalls.'

'He's booked. You do the show.'

The curtain went up. I was first on, as John Evans, the Welshman. I started singing my song.

I stopped singing and looked at this one little man in the auditorium. He wasn't even in the best seat.

I said, 'sir, you've paid to see the show. But what would you rather? To sit there on your own and watch it. Or you could come to the pub now and have a pint and a ploughman's lunch. And we'll give you another ticket to see the show tonight. What do you reckon?'

'That's a good idea.' We took him out to lunch and he saw the show in the evening.

I was tested severely that tour with forbidden fruit. We were playing the Adeline Genee Theatre in East Grinstead for a week. Next door to the theatre was the Bush-Davies Ballet School. After school came out at four o'clock the girls would come round to the theatre and to the dressing-room in their school uniforms. They wanted to hang with real professional actors (us!). We gave them tea and they asked us about make-up and touring and so on. A couple of the girls latched on to me and a couple on to Bill and a couple on to Roy, one of the stage managers. After the Friday night show this half dozen were waiting outside the stage door. We had already given them autographs and so on, so I said, 'What's happening girls?'

'Shh!' My two girls grabbed me by the hands and pulled me towards the bushes. I looked over my shoulder and Bill and Roy were being similarly abducted. 'What's going on?'

'We've sneaked out of school.'

'Yes, but why?'

They looked at each other. Then one said, 'We've never kissed anybody. But you're an actor. You must have done it thousands of times.'

'I suppose so.'

The blonde husky one said, 'Well, will you kiss me?'

'All right.'

So I kissed her.

Then the other one said, 'What about me?'

So I kissed her as well. Suddenly they said, 'Shh!' and put their torches out. One of their teachers was coming. I could see the light of the teacher's flashlight coming towards me in the bushes. I looked at the two girls who I could see faintly in the moonlight, two girls in school uniforms and in my mind's eye I could see the doors to Pentonville Prison swinging open for me.

The teacher passed us by and I breathed again.

'I think you'd better go, girls, before we all get into trouble.'

'All right.'

They both kissed me on the cheek and skipped off back to school. I emerged from the bush and found Bill looking about as shaken as I was.

I looked at Bill and he looked at me.

'Pentonville?' I said.

'No, Walton,' he replied.

There was no sign of Roy and his two girls. The next day he was full of stories, but I think it was just big talk. I'm fairly sure he was as frightened as Bill and I were.

I was asked by Granada Television if I would like to do an episode of a brand new series called *Seasons of the Year*. The star of the show was to be a house. It would start in the fifteenth century and every episode a hundred years would have passed. I jumped at the chance. In the cast was the lovely (here I go again!) Diana Sheridan and the great Thora Hird. I was also reunited with one of my colleagues from *Doctor Who*, Wendy Padbury. I was playing Jethro, the stable lad who was in love with the daughter of the house, played by Jaquie Stanbury. Donald Hewlitt was also in the cast, long before he made his name as the Colonel in *It Aint Half Hot, Mum*.

We had great fun on that show rehearsing near the Oval. There was nowhere to eat nearby so I would bring a bottle of wine, Diana Sheridan would bring some ham, Thora would bring cheese and Wendy would bring bread and we had picnic in the rehearsal room for lunch.

We went up to shoot the studio stuff in Manchester. One night Wendy and Jacqui and I went out for a meal and had great fun and I took them back to my hotel room for a nightcap from the minibar. *There was a rap on the door. Uh oh – it's the hotel detective, or a manager; we're making too much noise.*

I opened the door. There in her nightdress and curlers was Thora Hird. She spoke in an imperious tone. 'What's going on?'

'Well, Thora, me and the girls were having a bit of a party …'

'I know it's a party,' said Thora, chilling me to the bone. 'I can hear the giggling and the whooping and the jumping on the bed! I can tell it's a party!' And then she beamed. 'Why wasn't I invited?'

I put my arms around her and gave her a big hug.

'Thora, you are always welcome to our parties. Come on in.'

She wouldn't come in that time because she had to be on set first thing in the morning for a big scene, but she made us promise that she'd be there next time. I kissed her on both cheeks and she went to bed. I met Thora many times since then and she was one of those ladies who always seemed to bring sunshine into the lives of those around her. Thora died on 15 March 2003 and I really miss her. She truly was an amazing lady with an incredible sense of humour. I even suggested taking her to the pictures one evening to see her latest film, about the Japanese attack on Pearl Harbour.

'I'm not in that, love!'

I said, 'You must be. It's called *Thora! Thora! Thora!*' and she laughed.

All the outside filming for *Seasons of the Year* was done at Rudding House, just outside Harrogate in Yorkshire – the home of Sir Everard Radcliffe – and it was lovely to be back in my native Yorkshire. In a sense it will always be home to me. I was very pleased to be visiting the county again. But I didn't dream that I was about to commence the best part of twenty years there.

Chapter Six
When *Emmerdale* was just
an Allotment

Yes that's the gag. *I knew Emmerdale Farm when it was just an allotment.* And yes, it was a simpler place in the beginning. Planes didn't fall on the farm in those days. You'd be more likely to see a knitting circle than a lesbian love triangle. In fact, I knew *Emmerdale Farm* when they were planting seeds, because of course I was part of the original cast. I was recruited in the planning stages back in 1972.

I was having lunch with Liza Goddard and her parents down at Wrecclesham Farm at Farnham in Surrey. Liza and I had split up a long time before this but we had been friends since we were eleven years old and that hadn't changed.

I asked Liza's dad, David, what he was up to at the moment and he said he was producing a new afternoon show for ITV about a farming family.

'I've cast most of it,' he said. 'I've got a mother, the older son and the sister but I can't find quite anybody for the younger brother.'

'Daddy,' said Liza. 'You're looking at him. Frazer's ideal. He was born in Yorkshire and can do the Yorkshire accent.'

David looked at me thoughtfully. I had worked for him before, when I was no' but a lad.

'That's right Frazer. You were born in Yorkshire. Leave it with me.'

But Liza hadn't finished. 'In fact Daddy, if you don't give Frazer the part, Mummy and I will leave home!'

Two days later I was sitting with Muriel Cole and Sue Whatmough, the casting directors for *Emmerdale Farm*, at Yorkshire Television. I already knew Muriel because I had auditioned for a part in *Follyfoot*. Hang on, you're thinking, I don't remember Frazer Hines in *Follyfoot*.

True. Because I wasn't in it.

Muriel thought I'd be right for it and she sent me to the programme's producer, Francis Essex. Taking the part would mean moving to Yorkshire for six months, which was how long the show was supposed to run. It was a week later that I actually got to meet Francis. I had my bags packed and practically had my ticket for the trip north. Francis spent ninety minutes with me, and at the end of the interview he said, 'Sorry, Frazer, you're wrong.'

'About what.'

'Wrong for the part.'

To say I was surprised is to suggest that Vlad the Impaler was bad-tempered. 'How do you mean, "wrong for the part"?'

Well, look, I've spoken to you now for about an hour and a half and what strikes me most strongly is that your eyes twinkle and you have a lovely smile.'

So I said, 'Well, yes; that's me. I've been telling you what I've been up to. And I'm enjoying myself.'

Francis took on a patient tone. 'You see, your character, Steve, this boy never smiles, he has sad eyes. It says so in the script.'

I had read the script. 'Well that's the character. Give me the script and I'll play him.'

'But you smile too much.'

'*I* do, yes. Frazer smiles,' I answered, 'but Steve doesn't. Francis, think it through: if I was playing a rapist, would you want me to grab your secretary and throw her across the desk with my hands on her throat. It's called acting.'

But he would have none of it, so I didn't get the part; which as it happens, was probably fortuitous for me. If I'd been in *Follyfoot* I wouldn't have been sitting there again talking to Muriel and Sue about *Emmerdale Farm*.

They asked me what I knew about farming and I blithely told them that I used to know some farming people in Yorkshire years and years ago. Was that good enough? Oh dear, Frazer, perhaps that was not exactly what they wanted to hear.

'Everybody knows farming people. That's not quite the same thing as knowing about farming.'

'I used to know them quite well …' They shook their heads. OK: did I know how to cast a fly, because young Joe Sugden started off as a fly-fisherman?

'Oh yes,' I bluffed. 'Fly-fishing? Me? Constantly! Rod never out of my hand. Every morning and weekend in the season …' (Is there a season for fly-fishing? I decided to assume there was.)

It worked. Kevin Laffan, the creator of *Emmerdale Farm*, smiled, shook my hand and that was it.

I got a call from my agent the very next day. 'They liked you. The job's yours. Yesss!'

The new cast was contracted for thirteen episodes, which was the industry standard for this kind of afternoon programme. Granada had *Crown Court*, Thames Television had *Marked Personal* and *Harriet's Back in Town* and ATV had *General Hospital*, which were all made for the afternoon schedule and tailored to suit a mid-afternoon audience.

I was getting used to packing my bags for the trip up north, but this time it was work. I threw my worldly possessions into my little Morris 1300 GT and was off to Yorkshire.

Yorkshire Television had booked me into the Highfield Hotel, just up the road from the studio in Leeds. I arrived at the Highfield looking forward with excitement to the job which was due to start the following morning with our first read through of the script.

Now, I'm the kind of actor who believes that there's nothing worse on stage or screen than playing a character in a costume that doesn't feel appropriate. The clothes have to feel right for the character: it's one of the ways to get the performance right. This was certainly true for Joe Sugden. He was supposed to be a young but seasoned country boy. I envisaged going out with the wardrobe department and them kitting me out with brand new shirts and trousers, fresh out of the manufacturer's cellophane. Because that's what Joe would wear to go fishing, isn't it …? No, I didn't think so either. So I brought up some old clothes of my own that I thought would suit the character of Joe.

I left the clothes with the wardrobe department, who were delighted, and went back to reception where Sue Dumbell, the director's assistant, collected us and took us all upstairs to the YTV board-room where we opened our briefcases, brought out the very first *Emmerdale Farm* scripts and sat at the table. A very studious floor-manager type chap came in. Glasses. Tall. Flustered. Pencil behind the ear. Definitely the floor manager. Or stage manager. A man with a mission at any rate.

'Hello,' he said. 'I'm Andrew Burt. I'm playing Jack Sugden.'

Oops! My brother. I looked at him. My *tall* brother. Could have sworn it was the floor manager. Good thing I didn't ask him to get a cup of tea.

Next to arrive was David Goddard, followed by the directors. I had worked with Tristan de Vere Cole before on *Doctor Who*, so I knew him. The other director at that time was Gordon Flemyng, a wiry Scot, who I also knew from a film we had worked on. I think it was *Just for Fun* with Cherry Roland in 1963.

Gordon said to me at the time, 'Young man; I'm going to make you a star one day!', which was very kind of him.

I looked around the room at the other cast members of *Emmerdale Farm*. There was Sheila Mercier, who was to play Annie Sugden, Freddie Pyne, Arthur Pentelow and Andrew Burt. Toke Townley was to play my granddad, Sam Pearson. Toke was a genuine and lovable old character in life as well as on screen. We all missed him dreadfully when he died. And of course there was Gail Harrison who was to play Marion Wilks.

No script is absolutely perfect and an actor will always want to make it his own. I'll give you a 'for instance'.

Joe had a line when he was talking about his fly-fishing. 'If I'd just waited another second, I'd have had that little fellow.' But the line sounded about as right to me in Joe's mouth as him wearing new clothes.

On the read-through I said, 'If I'd just waited another second I'd have had the little bugger.'

'David Goddard was out of his chair in a second. 'Er, no, no, no. You can't say "bugger" on afternoon television Frazer!'

Not the way he said it you can't.

'But that's how I'd speak,' I answered. I offered it to him with a thick Yorkshire accent. 'How about "booger"?'

'You can't say "bugger", however you pronounce it.'

'Ok. I'll say. "I'd have had the little bas…"'

'You can't say that either.'

'"The little sod"…?'

'No!'

'No sods?'

'No sods. No bastards and no buggers.'

'David,' I said. 'I thought I was allowed one bum and two titties per script.'

'Not on afternoon television.'

'Well how about … Can I call him a little swine?'

A beatific smile spread across his face. '"Swine" is fine. "Swine" is acceptable. "Swine" is beautiful.'

The rest of the cast were all staying at the Highfield Hotel, so that night we all went out together to a Chinese restaurant to get to know each other a little. It's good to see if you like each other and we did. In fact, we got on so famously that I knew we'd have a great time and I began to think that the programme might be a bit special even then. The preliminary nerves melted away and I settled down to sleep the sleep of the tired.

The next morning found us all piling into the minibus to drive up to the beautiful Yorkshire village of Arncliffe. The whole village must have thought they were having a close encounter of the third kind. There were caravans and wardrobe vans, catering units and film and sound crew. It is nothing less than an invasion when a large crew pulls into town and it inevitably causes quite a stir with the locals. But everyone was really friendly and of course no one knew what the programme was. We weren't on air yet.

The first scene we had to shoot was the funeral of my father, Jacob, so we all changed into mourning suits and assembled outside the church.

Suddenly we heard the whir of a helicopter. The chopper circled over our heads and settled on the village green. We all looked at each other – was there a rich Sugden cousin we hadn't been told about?

Out of the helicopter and ducking under the slowing rotor-blades stepped a handsome Arab gentleman in a brown leather jacket, tight trousers, black gloves and sunglasses. We held our breath. There was a pause and then he spoke.

'Hello. I Mustapha cameraman. I you come to shoot,' he said. 'With film of course!'

We all fell about laughing.

So this was to be our cameraman Mustapha Hamouri. Soon to be award-winning cameraman for all the Hannah Hauxwell documentaries such as 1973's *Too Long a Winter*. He set his camera up in the village while we were driving around in the Dales in our funeral cortege. We parked in a lay-by, waiting for our cue to move. Sitting inside my hearse was Sheila, Toke, Freddie and Jo Kendall (playing my sister Peggy). I cracked a gag and we all laughed, just as a car came round the corner. The look on that car's passenger's faces as they saw a funeral car with everyone laughing like drains was a picture. So we had an idea. Every time a car came past we laughed. We had such fun waiting for our cue – and we saw so many wonderfully disgusted faces!

After our first night of filming we stayed at the Falcon Inn. It was a lovely pub. You probably know it – only you know it as the Woolpack. It was owned by Amos Brearley back then and has been one of the great constants of the series. We've been so used to it being the Woolpack for twenty-four years now.

That first night the Falcon had plenty of accommodation for us, but there was competition, as there always is for the best room. In this case it was the one with the four-poster bed.

'I'm your mother,' Sheila Mercier said. 'I hope my boys know how to treat their mother.'

And we did. Sheila got the room with the four-poster bed.

We wined and dined and quaffed countless bottles of the red stuff. There was a distinct party atmosphere. Tristan and Gordon, our two directors, were trading toasts with Keith Richardson, who is now the executive producer of *Emmerdale* and head of drama at YTV, but who was then the floor manager.

'Here's to Keith!', 'Here's to Tristan!', 'Here's to getting up tomorrow morning and going back to work …!'

Whoops! Quite right. So we all trooped upstairs, chastened by the thought of filming tomorrow with a hang-over. But that wasn't the end of the night. It was all innocent high-jinks really. A lot of giggling and whooping and dashing in and out of the make-up girls' rooms and hiding under beds and grabbing their ankles when they came back from the loo. It was a combination of Greyfriars and St Trinian's.

Finally, when things were getting totally out of hand, a voice bellowed out from another room: It was Sheila.

'What's going on Freddie Pyne?'

I looked out of my bedroom and there was Freddie tiptoeing along with a pair of underpants on his head and a chair which he was about to jam under the handle of someone's room to lock them in. He looked round guiltily, exactly like a naughty schoolboy who has been caught by the headmistress.

'Just what do you think you're doing?' Sheila shouted. 'And why has nobody wrecked my room yet?'

We all burst out laughing and went off to sleep.

Mustapha Hamouri and I have been friends ever since that day. His English has improved considerably since 1972 but that doesn't stop me pulling his leg. He tried to teach me a little of his language once, or at least how to count up to ten in Arabic. We got as far as 'Och, ach, ich, lech, habas …' and then he was enraged when I said 'OK. I know it all the way up to ten now.'

'What you mean? I not teach you yet!'

'I don't need you to teach me the rest.'

Musti was puzzled, 'Why not? Tell Mustapha.'

'Och, ach, ich, lech, habas, sphinx, camel, pyramid, Taureg, Bedouin,' I answered.

Mustapha was not impressed by this. 'No, no, no, Frazer. You all the time putting the mickey into me.' And he was right. I all the time am. But he knows that I tease him because I love him.

He is also a very thorough cameraman. No matter how brilliant we had been, if there was any kind of technical hitch, Musti would want to do it over again. We would do a complicated scene with long speech and we would get it in the can and the director would shout 'Cut!' But Musti would point out that the sun had gone behind a cloud.

'I think it looks better if sun shines on face and everything looks wonderful.' He would give us his most beguiling smile and we would think, yes, it will look better if everything is wonderful. Who were we to argue with a genius in the making?

One day we were at Arthur Peel's farm when one of the props men came running up to David Green, now a Hollywood director, who cut his teeth on *Emmerdale Farm*.

'David,' the man said in breathless excitement. 'The farmer said Daisy's about to calf …'

'Tell me that Daisy is a cow,' David answered.

But the fellow was too excited to get the joke. 'Why don't we dash over there with Frazer, Freddy and Musti and film it? It would look great if we stick it in a later episode.'

'Actually, that is a very good idea,' David said.

We rushed over and there was the cow in all her glory with the calf half poking out. Freddy and I hurried in, tied a rope around its forelegs and heaved and pulled like the Wakefield Hospital Maternity Ward tug-o-war team. All the while Musti was walking around filming us with a hand-held camera. Eventually the calf fell to the ground. We broke the bag and cleaned it off and David said, 'Great, wonderful, marvellous; have a cigar. How was it for you Musti?'

Without thinking Musti said, 'I think to do one more take.'

So I looked at Musti and I looked at David and I looked at Wilf.

'OK, Wilf, lads – stick the calf back in the cow!'

Without batting an eyelid the prop boys picked up the calf and Mustapha giggled and said, 'Oh no of course, I no can do it.'

I think everybody in the cast and crew of *Emmerdale Farm* had an enormous fondness for Gail Harrison, who played Marion Wilks. She was a wonderful looking girl and I freely admit that I too was just a little bit smitten.

It must have been on the third or fourth day of filming, in the evening after a couple of bottles of Beaujolais, that she suggested we all walk to the top of a mountain not far from where we were. It didn't look far, so off we went.

It was a lovely, gentle summer's evening. A small crowd of us strolled towards the mountain, enjoying the company and the scenery. As we went, I kept an eye on the people we were losing here and there along the way and secretly promised myself that I was there for the duration. There was no way I was dropping out, not with Gail as possible first prize at the end of the hike!

Sure enough, by the time we reached the summit of the hill, puffing and panting, only Gail and I were left of the company which had set out. We shared a laugh at the ones who hadn't made it and turned round to see the most magnificent sunset happening just for us. We sank into lush summer grass to watch the sun and moon change place and I thought to myself, this is the stuff that romantic novels are made of! We leaned against one another, transfixed by the sinking sun setting the horizon on fire and I could feel the warmth of her body against my shoulder. I turned and looked into her eyes and she gazed back into mine and said …

'It's getting dark, Frazer. We ought to be getting back.'

Curses! I thought: *Hines, you're losing your touch.*

But Gail was the kind of girl you didn't want to take advantage of. We strolled down the mountain hand in hand, diverted for a moment by glow-worms in the twilight, lined up in two ranks like an airport landing strip. It was a magical evening, although when we got back to the hotel there was a certain amount of vulgar raising of eyebrows amongst those still drinking at the bar. We went to our rooms with a virtuous sense of our own innocence. Nothing had happened.

I soon got bored of staying at the Highfield Hotel so I rented a flat at Brentwood Court. David Green had moved in there and eventually Sheila moved there too, as did Gail. It soon became known as 'Emmerdale Court'.

One night I was having a quiet evening in and there was a knock at the door. It was Gail.

'May I come in?' she said.

Well of course she could. I still had the feeling that we missed a chance up on the mountain.

I gave her a glass of wine and a chair and sat on the floor at her feet. I was a little worried about her. I was used to a lively, bubbly Gail, but this girl was quiet and troubled.

'What's the matter, Gail? You can tell me.'

'I'm very lonely,' she sighed.

That was easy to understand. She had recently lost her mother, to whom she had been very close, She wasn't sleeping.

I was listening to Elgar's 'Enigma Variations'. I put a pillow down and we lay on the floor together and let the music drift over us. Under the circumstances it didn't occur to me to try to seduce her and instead we became very close friends who never went any further than a stolen kiss behind the set. She soon found a boyfriend in London and then our innocent kisses came to an end.

Sue Dumbell came in one day when we were rehearsing back in Leeds and sat with us waiting for a natural break in the action so that she could break the news.

'Listen,' she told us. 'I've just seen our schedules and we're going to Episode 26.'

You can imagine our elation. Great! Another thirteen weeks work! I'd already had one scare. At the end of episode 9, Joe was in a car crash and wasn't expected to live. I couldn't wait for the script of Episode 10 to arrive on my doorstep. I opened it: 'Joe's in intensive care'. Episode 11: 'Joe's getting better'. And so it went on until he was fit again. The rest, as they say, is history. Who'd have thought, though, that twenty years later, Joe's car would be involved in a similar accident that would seal his fate?

About six months into the serial Patricia Haines arrived as Squire Verney's wife, Laura. Squire Verney was to be played by that old film actor, Patrick Holt, who arrived in our midst every inch the film star in his silver Rolls-Royce, with his grey moustache and grey, slicked-back wavy hair. Patricia was a very attractive, warm lady and we took a shine to her immediately. She and I became good friends very quickly.

One day during a tea break she was showing me some photographs, including some of a ravishing girl. I picked one up. 'Who's this?'

Patricia was suddenly alert. 'That's my daughter, Nikki.'

Nikki was the product of Patricia's marriage to Michael Caine, with whom I had worked on the film *The Last Valley*.

'Patsy, she's lovely!'

'Hands off, Frazer. She's only fifteen,' said Patricia detaching the photo from my grip.

'It's OK Patsy. I know how to behave myself.' I said, properly wary of the protective mother. 'But when she reaches sixteen you must introduce us!'

Patsy finished her stint in *Emmerdale Farm* and away she went. But *Emmerdale Farm* went from strength to strength. Twenty-six episodes became fifty-two and *Emmerdale Farm* was well on its way to becoming the much-loved television institution it is today.

My only relationship at that time was with a young actress called Seretta, in London, and it was beginning to wane. It finally crashed when it came into conflict with my love of horses.

I had met a trainer in Harrogate called Steve Nesbitt who became a firm friend. Steve was a Yorkshire trainer and I was carrying a book called *Horses In Training*. Steve tapped me on the shoulder and said, 'Young man, I see you are carrying a copy of *Horses In Training*. That's not a normal gambler's book.'

'No, I'm just looking up two trainers I used to ride for, Scobie Breasley and Ron Smyth, to see if the same horses are in training.'

'Well, come and ride out for me then; I'm at Newby Hall,' he said.

We swapped phone numbers and two days later he phoned me to ride out. The horse he put me on was an old plodder called Wee Game. I jumped on it and Steve told me to follow the rest of the string of riders. I followed the string on a nice easy canter until we entered the final straight. Wee Game then changed gear. I tried to wrestle with him but to no avail: he had run off with me. Fetch me the *Sporting Life*, said one of the wags as I passed him. I tried to turn Wee Game in ever-decreasing circles, but the early morning dew made it very slippy for him and we came down together and rolled over in a heap. I jumped up and grabbed his reins as Steve came running up.

'Are you all right?'

'Yes, sorry Steve, but the bugger just ran off with me.'

'Are you walking back or should I leg you up?'

'No, leg me up. I'll ride him back.'

Steve legged me up into the saddle, I got my feet into the stirrups and we trotted off home. Over breakfast Steve looked at me and said, 'Well lad, you'll do for me.'

'How do you mean?' I asked.

'After a fall like that most people would have walked away, it may have even finished their riding careers, but not you. You can come again.'

After I'd ridden out for him a few times, he had a surprise for me. He had written to the Licensing Department of the Jockey Club and got me a jockey's licence. I could now ride in a race! My first competitive ride was on a filly called Wingate Lass. We made all the running and finished last! But it was a start … now I had to have my own horse. I bought a grey filly called Avocet Tracy.

At the time I had become friends with Ted Hemsley who played football for Sheffield United and also playing cricket for Worcestershire.

'I'll have a share of that horse, Frazer. We'll share it between us,' Ted suggested.

She ran quite a few times for us, never won but was placed two or three times. Eventually we sold her to be a point to pointer.

'Ted,' I said. 'I've found another horse.'

'No. Count me out.'

'But this is a good one,' I told him. 'Steve's just bought this one out of a seller on the flat. He's going to be really good. He's called Ingham.'

But Ted wouldn't be moved. 'No. My wife doesn't want me to share another horse.'

So I discussed the possibilities with Seretta of me still buying the half share if Steve retained the other half. Seretta on the other hand wanted us to get engaged (me and her, not me and the horse). I had about £500 saved with which I planned to buy her an engagement ring. But now I had the opportunity of buying a half share in Ingham, who would cost the same.

Steve was convinced that Ingham would win races. If it did win, then I would have prize money and that would mean I could buy an even bigger engagement ring. This seemed like a pretty sound plan to me and I put it to Seretta. It didn't appear to impress her a great deal. She put her foot down: an engagement ring – now – or nothing.

No man should ever have to make such a choice. I really wanted that horse …

So Seretta and I went our separate ways and Ingham went on to win thirteen races for Steve and I. Old Ingham enabled me to buy Excavator Lady, who started my horse-breeding business. She was a wonderful bomb-proof mare to ride at home and in races.

Sometime later Patsy Haines returned to *Emmerdale Farm*. We were delighted to have her back, so when one day she said, 'Frazer would you like to take me out to supper?'

I naturally said, 'I'd be glad to, Patsy.'

'Pick me up at the Highfield at eight o'clock.'

I duly arrived, rang the doorbell and kissed Patsy hello when she opened the door. Then she said, 'I've got a surprise for you, Frazer. Meet Nikki.'

She stepped aside and there behind her stood a ravishing blonde-haired, blue-eyed, trainee goddess. She stepped forward. 'So, you're the fellow I wasn't to meet until I was sixteen,' Nikki said.

'I did promise you could meet her when she was old enough,' said Patsy.

I left Highfield with a lady on each arm, feeling about as pleased as a puppy with two tails. I couldn't believe my luck. Here I was, Frazer Hines, taking two of the most beautiful women I had ever seen in my life out to supper. I ordered champagne.

'Oo, Mimin!' said Nikki (that was what she called her mum). 'Plonk de plonk!'

At the end of the night I said to Nikki, 'Do you fancy coming out again another night?'

'Well, yes. I'm here for another few days with mum. I'd love to.'

Patsy was gracious. 'Don't mind me! Go ahead.'

So we went out to the pictures a couple of times and swapped phone numbers and I began to think: this girl could be special, but she's very young.

Nikki wanted to be a show-jumper and was living with her trainer Marion Mould down at Blindley Heath in Sussex. She rang me one day to say, 'Marion's having a party this weekend. Would you like to come down for it?'

Would I ever!

On Friday night I finished work at the studio and drove all the way down to their house near Gatwick Airport, which was a good 200 miles. The party was a great success and I met a couple who figure high on my personal list of heroes, Marion and David Mould. We all danced and fooled the night away and then, when the party was winding down and people were beginning to drift away, Nikki appeared at my side and whispered into my ear.

'Would you like to step into the garden with me for a minute?'

My heart leapt and I let her take my hand and lead me outside. I felt a little bit of the excitement of a schoolboy on his first date; it was almost enough just to be alone with this girl holding her hand. We stood looking out at the night and she leaned her head on my shoulder and said, 'Can you see Caernarfon?'

Now geography may not be my strongest suit, but even I know Caernarfon is up in the top left-hand corner of Wales and you'd need reflecting telescope to see if from Blindley Heath.

'Caernarfon … my horse.'

Oh I see. Caernarfon's a horse! 'No. No, I can't …'

'He's out there somewhere. Come on, Narvy, come on. Where are you?'

The wind was getting up and it was dark and I couldn't see the horse so when she said, 'He must be asleep', I let her take me back inside without making a move on her.

While I was beginning to see quite a lot of Nikki – and found myself thinking about seeing even more of her – I didn't know whether she thought of me as a sort of older brother, or just a friend of her mother's, or as a friend with whom she shared a mutual interest in horses. I was, after all, quite a lot older than her.

I decided I had to put it to the test. Not to test Nikki but to test my own feelings for her. I'd get her away from Marion and David's for a day and take her riding at Frensham Ponds – a place where I rode often and which was special to me.

I took her to Mrs Carter's riding school and found two of her finest horses. Mrs Carter always had great horses at Frensham Ponds. And we went for a long ride across the top of the Beacon. We pulled up breathless at the summit and leapt out of the saddle.

'Let's give the horses a breather,' I suggested.

We were breathing pretty heavily ourselves; there's nothing so exhilarating as a good ride to the top of a deserted hill.

This was the moment of truth. I took hold of both of Nikki's hands and tried to catch her eyes, but she looked away. But then she turned her head back and looked at me.

'You look very cold,' I said.

'I am a bit.'

I put my arms around her and pulled her close to me and she came in close lifting her face up to mine. Our lips met. Her lips were softer – and colder! – than any lips I ever kissed and I knew that I had made my mind up about her.

But I didn't want to force my attentions on her, so I pulled back a little. She opened her eyes and the message in them was that she wanted me to kiss her again. So I did. And that was the start of three very happy years with Nikki.

Patsy was over the moon when she heard that her little bit of matchmaking had worked. I thought Nikki's father, Michael Caine, might be less thrilled. But Nikki said that she would handle her dad and it would be all right. She went to see him to break the news.

'Dad,' said Nikki. 'I met this actor.'

'Oh yeah?' answered Michael.

'I'm in love with him.'

'Oh yeah?'

'And he's in love with me.'

'Yeah, he would be. So who is it?'

'Well,' said Nikki. 'He says he knows you.'

'Oh yeah?'

'Apparently you made a film together in 1970 in Austria.'

'1970? That would be … *The Last Valley*.' One Caine eyebrow was perceptibly raised.

'That's the one. He says you got on really well together. It's Frazer Hines.'

'Oh yeah?'

Nikki held her breath.

'Yes,' said Michael. 'I know him. Nice lad, He's all right. And thank God if you find yourself an actor, you found one who loves horses. When are going to bring him down then?'

So two days later I went to supper, which is an institution in Michael's house. He's the most wonderful person to be in the company of. He's a genius and a generous host. And he doesn't care who you are. Millionaire or ordinary bloke, if you're friends of his you all sit down at the table together. I remember lots of suppers at his house with Harry Saltzman, Roger Moore and Nikki and I.

Although Michael had smiled on our relationship I was still nervous of one phone call I had to make. My summer holidays had come round and Mustapha and his lovely wife Jill, along with a few technicians, their wives, and I had rented a villa on Corfu. (This was before Corfu became lager-lout central.) Naturally, Nikki wanted to come to.

'Well, I don't know, Nikki. I don't suppose your father will let you come away with me like that.'

'But he knows we're in love. Ask him. Call him and ask him.'

'Ooh, Nikki. I couldn't do that. I'm not asking him.'

'Don't be such a pussy!'

'Couldn't you ask him?' I said.

'I can't. You'll have to.'

I made the call.

'Michael, it's Frazer. Look, we've got this villa in Corfu for a month and Nikki wants to come too. Can I take her away on holiday?'

There was a longish pause and I thought, *Oh, Frazer, you've gone too far this time.*

Finally, Michael said, 'If you do take her away, you will look after her, won't you Frazer?'

I said, 'Of course I will Michael. I love her very much.'

'You know what I mean, Frazer. "Look after her".'

I said, 'Yes, Michael. I do know what you mean. I'll look after her.'

'OK. She can go.'

'Thank you, Michael.'

I knew what he was talking about and I brought Nikki home safe and sound.

Nikki and I weren't living together but we managed to spend practically every weekend together. She would come up to my house in Chiswick and I would drive down from Yorkshire. And at 6 am on Monday morning I would kiss my mother and Nikki both goodbye and they would stand on the doorstep in their dressing-gowns waving me off. It was an awful wrench, let me tell you.

Or, on the weekends when Nikki was riding at a show I would go and stay with her and Marion and David. David and I both had these white, sheepskin jackets and it was our practice to warm up the horses while Nikki and Marion walked the course. One day we were walking the horses round the paddock, just keeping them warm, in our matching jackets, when I heard a couple of onlookers say, 'My, that Marion Mould's got a lot of money, you know?'

'How do you make that out, then?'

'Well, look, she's got David Mould and Frazer Hines working for her and they're just grooms!'

Back on the *Emmerdale Farm* front we were seeing a few changes. David Goddard, our original producer, was no longer with us. A new man had taken over, Peter Holmans, who held the fort for a while. And then, in turn, he handed over to his successor, Robert D Cardona.

Bob made one hell of an entrance. Tall. Jet-black hair swept back. Viva Zapata moustache. Long wolf-skin coat. This was our new producer? But he was a lovely man and we all took to him and his wife, Gloria Tors, in no time. I was especially delighted with Gloria, who wrote some terrific humorous scenes for me in *Emmerdale Farm*.

On day I said to Gloria and Bob, 'Look, can't we get a bit of spice for Joe. He hasn't got anybody in his love life. Couldn't we have some glamorous women in the show?'

'Waall,' said Bob in his slow American drawl. 'We'll have to think about that.'

'Somebody like Jenny Hanley,' I said. 'She's beautiful. See if you can get a Jenny Hanley type. That's what we need.'

Bob and Gloria looked doubtful, so I left it at that. About three months later I turned up on set for a scene with a girl coming into the show for a few episodes. The character had to get out of her car and say, 'Hello, Joe. I'm Bridy Middleton. I've come to bid you at your sheep.'

I got to the location and changed and was called, not by the call boy, but by the producer. Bob, who was also directing (he was a brilliant director) knocked on the caravan door.

'Frazer, are ready for the scene?'

'Yes, Bob.'

'Come this way then. It's your birthday today isn't it?'

'That's right. How did you know?'

'I've got a little present for you. There you go.' And he pointed at this white MG. 'Happy Birthday!'

Out of the car stepped Jenny Hanley.

'Hello, Joe Sugden. I'm Bridy Middleton. I've come to bid you at your sheep.'

Thanks Bob. That was my present. Jenny Hanley in *Emmerdale Farm*. And as Bob put it, 'Why settle for a Jenny Hanley type if you can have Jenny Hanley herself?'

But it was too late. I was already in love with Nikki. Still, Jenny and I did become firm friends and we actually posed for a *TV Times* feature, 'Your Ideal Picnic Partner'. Working with Jenny was one of the many pleasures of being in *Emmerdale Farm*.

Nikki and I spent three years together and even now I still have some regrets about her. Perhaps we should have got married, but she was very young. Actually, she wanted us to get engaged, but for once I felt that instead of *me* being too young to settle down, *she* was. When it came to it, I said. 'Go off and live for a bit Nikki. Have some fun. Maybe in a year's time or so we'll meet up and then we'll get married.'

As a fortune-teller I was nearly on the mark. Off she went. She had some fun. She fell in love. She did get married. But not to me!

Chapter Seven
They Were Playing Our Song

Emmerdale Farm was going from strength to strength. Some really good people were appearing in it, more than a few of whom have since become very famous. Louise Jameson, who was later to battle evil throughout space and time wearing a leather bikini in *Doctor Who* playing Leela, was murdered. Joanne Whalley (later Whalley-Kilmer after marrying Val Kilmer), now an international film star, was raped. Anna Friel, before she starred in *Brookside*, had the love-sick blues for Joe Sugden, as Poppy Bruce. And Lesley Manville wet herself …

Perhaps I should explain.

It was one of Lesley's first television jobs and she was a delight to work with. But I couldn't help teasing her. I had a scene with her where I had to dash in and announce that Daisy the cow was about to calve. And then get her to put some hot water on, for a cup of tea.

We rehearsed the scene. I was already dressed as Joe Sugden in jeans and a check shirt. When we were ready for a take I went outside where I had primed the wardrobe department to have a white jacket ready for me which I put on back to front, and a surgeon's mask, a hat and rubber gloves.

Wearing this outlandish garb I dashed back in, 'Quick, Daisy's about to calve. Boil some water!' Lesley turned round, took one look at me, and dropped the teapot.

'Oh god, Frazer. I don't believe it! Look, I've wet myself!'

Bob Cardona, who was directing, had a great sense of humour and he thought it was as funny as the rest of us did.

Some people really believe in their soaps. Andrew Burt had left the show by then for bigger and better things. Sheila Mercier received a letter once:

'Dear Annie, Your son, Jack, is not living in Italy – he's actually commanding a warship for the British Navy.'

This viewer had seen Andrew in the BBC series *Warship* and was convinced that Jack had joined the navy.

The producers wanted to bring Jack back, but Andrew didn't want to come back, so they recast him. Thus in 1980, four years after Andrew left, I had a new brother in Clive Hornby. I was very sad when Clive died in July 2008 of Hypoxia. (A medical condition that effectively starves the body of oxygen). Although we didn't live in each other's pockets and I'd left the show some years before, we were like real brothers. In fact, only the other day, somebody remarked that we were the Rosencrantz and Guildenstern of soap-opera.

I also had a new sister-in-law because Katie Barker, who played Dolly, had to leave for personal reasons. So in came Jean Rogers. It's always fun to rag a new member of cast. One day after rehearsal I snaffled Jean's script for the following day when she had a long scene and I wrote 'Cut' all across it. The next day when we came to do the scene she was completely perplexed.

'What's this?'

'It's a long scene, haven't you learnt it?'

'My script says it's cut.'

I let her stew for a few minutes and then owned up that it was Hines playing a practical joke.

The *Emmerdale* team were a very close-knit family. I'll give you an example. I was going off on holiday to Corfu with my girlfriend, Chris.

'Mind if I join you?' Sheila asked.

'No, of course not.'

Two days later I was paddling in the sea off Corfu and a stranger came up to me and said, 'We know who you are. We just wanted to tell you that your mother's arrived.'

I turned and there was Sheila standing at the water's edge beaming. I ran out and gave her a big hug. Well, she was my other mum, after all.

She had come with Anna Dawson, the great comedienne and singer. We had some marvellous raucous times in Corfu, the bunch of us. I tried to get Sheila to try one of the paragliders.

'Absolutely not, Frazer!' she said.

'How about you, Anna?'

'I don't think so.'

'Look, I'll show you, Anna, how easy it is.' And off I went round the bay with the parachute strapped to my back.

'Come on Anna, it's your turn now!' I yelled after I'd landed.

'No, I'm not doing it.'

'It's very easy. A piece of cake.'

'No,' she said, stepping into the harness.

'There's no point me holding the strap, Frazer. I'm not going.'

'Just put this buckle on your belt …'

'There's no point you buckling my belt.'

'That clips there.' I told her.

'Frazer, there's no need to clip that.' She insisted.

'When I say "run", run.'

'There's no point you saying "run", because I'm not running!"

'Run!' I said, and she started to run.

The boat went off. She jumped into the air with a great shriek. Within three seconds there was Anna, the old trouper, doing arabesques, grand jetes, tap routines and grinning. She was having a ball. Sheila, safe on terra firma, thought it was a hoot.

I love travelling. If I got a few days off I would go to a travel agent and find somewhere I could go on the spur of the moment. I went to Jersey that way and I shall always be glad I did because I met some people there who have remained friends throughout my life.

They were a husband and wife double act called The Krankies – Janette and Ian Tough. Both Scots. You probably know the act, where Janette dresses as a schoolboy and comes on to interrupt Ian's singing act, asking, 'Where's me mam?'

I saw them in cabaret one night on a trip to Jersey and laughed a lot at their act. Afterwards, Ian and Janette came to the bar where I was having a brandy. They introduced themselves – they were keen followers of *Emmerdale* – and invited me to join them for a picnic they were having the following day.

They took me to a little secluded cove where we laid out the picnic and sat in the sun.

'Who fancies a swim?' asked Ian.

Well I did and so did Janette. So we each took her by the hand and waded in to the channel. The water splashed up to our waists and then up to our chests and Ian and I were admiring the waves crashing over us when we heard a gurgling sound. We looked down and there was Janette completely submerged, with just her lips catching occasional breaths from the surface of the sea. Of course, Janette was a lot shorter than Ian and I. Oops! We pulled her back to shore, hoping we hadn't actually drowned her.

Ian had a little boat. 'We're going out to sea tomorrow, do you fancy joining us?'

'You bet!' I love the sea. My grandfather was many years before the mast and I can claim that the sea is in the Hines blood.

Next day I went down to the pier where the most delightful little cabin cruiser was bobbing on the water. We went out and the sea got rougher and rougher. Janette began to grow pale and she said, 'Ian, can we not head in now?'

'Yes, Ian,' I said. We should head back. I can see the newspaper headlines if we were to capsize. "Young TV star drowned with third-rate cabaret act".'

'You cheeky bugger! said Ian. We had immediately become firm friends.

Later on, when The Krankies' performance stole the Royal Variety Show, I sent them a telegram the next day, which read. "Brilliant Young Actor Now Recognises Third-Rate Cabaret Act As Top Of The Bill"!

If *Emmerdale* was like a family, then it was an extended family. As well as the actors and the production staff, I got to know most of the extras on the show. We used to enjoy swapping jokes between scenes. In particular there were two strapping lads, Roy Alon and John Lees. I met them when they were extras but they went on to become successful stuntmen, working on Bond movies and Pink Panther films. Sadly, both men died very young.

Roy came back to do a stunt on *Emmerdale*. We were doing a night shoot. Joe Sugden was out looking for some Christmas tree rustlers who were 'half-inching' his trees. Darrol Blake was the director and he was very concerned that we should wrap up the shoot by ten o'clock sharp, otherwise we would be paying mega-overtime.

The way to manage night shoots is that you wait until it is dark so that it looks like night and then you light the scene up so that the viewer can see what is happening. I know that sounds like a paradox, but you have to do it that way.

The idea was that I would dash into the road and a transit van would come towards me; there would be a camera in the van, shooting the scene from that point of view. Before the van hit me, Roy and I would change places – he would put on my jacket and trousers, we would shoot from another angle and the van would hit Roy and throw him into a ditch. Then we would change clothes again and the camera would focus on me in the ditch. Roll the title: is Joe alive or dead? Cliffhanger ending.

That was the plan. But the best laid plans of mice and men …

It got to half-past nine. We hadn't even started the scene. Roy came in to the caravan and said, 'Well, sunshine. I've got some good news and some bad news.'

'What's the good news?'

'We're ready to do the scene.'

'Great. Let's get on with it … Hang on. What's the bad news?'

'You've got to do your own stunt.'

'I've got to what!?'

'We don't have time, flower, to mess about changing costumes. You'll have to do it. It'll be all right. What we'll do is, I'll drive the van at you, we'll put a mark on the road where your left foot has to hit, and as the van passes you, you'll bang on the side of it and throw yourself backwards into the ditch. That's what I was going to do.'

Crikey! I thought. Do my own stunt! Is this a good idea? Stunt work is a professional business and the gung-ho amateur is a danger to all concerned. But I always like to try new things and I trusted Roy implicitly to look after me.

So I said, 'OK Roy, if you're happy about it. I'll do it.'

'Don't worry about it, Frazer,' said Roy. 'I'll be driving the truck. Just make sure your foot is on that mark on the road.'

The scene was set up. We rehearsed it once. If you get it wrong, somebody gets hurt. And this time it could be Hines!

It was ten to ten. Darrol was pacing up and down. 'We have to wrap at ten. We have to go for a take.'

'I'd like to rehearse it one more time,' said Roy.

'We don't have the time for a rehearsal and a take. We'll just have to go for it.'

'OK,' said Roy. 'We'll go for the take.'

Everybody took their positions. *Action!*

I dashed into the road. There was Roy coming towards me in the van. My foot found the marked spot in the road. The van passed me, missing my kneecap by the merest hair's width. I hit the side of the van, *BANG!* and threw myself back into the ditch. The hand-held camera came up for the close-up of Joe and the cliffhanger ending.

Roy came running up. 'Are you all right, Frazer?'

Thumbs up. It was one minute to ten. We had brought the scene in on schedule.

A week later Roy came to the set.

'Frazer, I've got a present for you. You're now an honorary member of Stunts Incorporated.'

This was Roy's team. He gave me a buckle with Stunts Inc on it and a blue bomber jacket with my name and the Stunts Inc logo. I was thrilled with them.

That gave me an idea. Most TV shows had sweat-shirts with the name of the show on them. I designed an *Emmerdale Farm* Stunt Team shirt – a flaming hoop with lots of little sheep diving through it, and the logo '*Emmerdale Farm* Stunt Team' underneath. I called Roy in turn and returned the compliment by presenting him with a sweat-shirt and a T-shirt to match.

Sometime later Roy went off to work with Robert Wagner. All the stuntmen on the project had their various sweat-shirts, from *Live and Let Die,* or *Moonraker* and Roy wore his *Emmerdale* shirt. Robert Wagner came over and said, 'What's this *Emmerdale Farm?*'

Roy explained that is was a TV soap in England. Robert said, 'Boy, I haven't got one of those sweat-shirts,' so Roy gave it to him. I love to think about Robert Wagner walking around Hollywood in an *Emmerdale Farm* sweat-shirt.

In fact Roy doubled for some of the biggest names in showbiz. Peter Sellers, Ryan O'Neill, O J Simpson, James Coburn, Sophia Loren – 'hang on,' you say, 'Sophia Loren?' Yes. In a 1979 film called *Firepower.* He sat on his chair with a wig to match Sophia's hair, a blouse and skirt, underneath which he wore a pair of tracksuit bottoms. It was time for the stunt.

'Oh Roy,' said Sophia. 'It is your time to double for me, but first you must take off your trousers.'

'Sophia, flower,' answered Roy. 'You've just satisfied a lifetime's ambition.'

'Oh really?' she enquired.

'Yes, to have Sophia Loren ask me to take my trousers off!'

Whenever I got some spare time I would go up to Scotland. I had discovered this marvellous place called the Eagle Hotel in Lauder, where you could go for a long weekend or a longer holiday and ride in the most beautiful countryside that Scotland could offer. The Eagle offered fabulous cuisine, comfortable beds and the kindest, gentlest horses you could wish for.

You'd trot down the road for two miles and turn left and the wrangler would take you to one side and point.

'You see that ruined farmhouse on the top of the hill about four miles away …? We'll gallop and see you there. If you want to jump go to the left; if you just want to gallop, take the track on the right.'

And off we would go, jumping hedges and fences and ditches. It was glorious. The Land Rover would come up at lunchtime and we'd find an old ruined bothy, which is a kind of farmhouse, where we'd take the saddles off and sit with a sandwich and a cold lager. All this, and the sun would be shining and the birds singing as well! Life was grand when the Eagle in Lauder was open for business.

You'll have gathered that I love a good practical joke, but it's a two-way street and I can be the butt of jokes as well as the instigator. I sometimes used to go to the Eagle Hotel with a friend – a mad Irish called John O'Loan. One time we went after a housewarming party when I moved from a little cottage in Little London, which is in Rawdon, near Leeds, round the corner to a slightly bigger cottage; I was buying more furniture and I needed the space. My girlfriend Chris had made a lovely big cake for me and we rather pushed the boat out. The eating and drinking went on longer than was strictly wise.

Which is why we were the worse for wear the next morning. Luckily John's lady, Sally, had been relatively abstemious, so we got in my Ford Granada and drove up to Lauder with John and me asleep in the back. When we got there word was already out that we were brutally hung-over. The first point of call should have been a cool and darkened bedroom, but the management were very keen that we should enjoy the equestrian facilities of the Eagle to the full. We were to go out riding that same afternoon.

'Don't worry, Frazer, we've got you a nice horse.'

A nice horse! I'll never forget that horse – his name is etched on my memory: McClusky. He pulled me all the way up the hill and down the other side. As his hooves pounded turf, the Rabelaisian dwarf in my head kept pounding my temples from the inside.

We went for a long gallop. I was trying to settle McClusky at the back, but he would have none of it. He was pulling and pulling. We came up to a huge fence. I didn't think I was going to make it. The wrangler pulled everybody to the side, to miss this fence out. But McClusky wanted to go for it. I had to pull on my right rein with both hands to make him go down the hill. Everybody had pulled up to look and just saw me heading off behind the dip. They all looked at each other. *Any minute now, there'll be an empty saddle coming up the hill.* They waited for a minute and then they heard a thunder of hooves and over the brow of the hill came McClusky with Hines clinging on for dear life. No doubt it looked very funny to the spectators but I didn't see the funny side of it until I had shaken my hangover and visited the hotel bar later that night. I headed McClusky for the knot of riders so that he would stop. My knuckles were scuffed from holding on to the mane on his neck.

I jumped off and said, 'Somebody else can ride this SOB. I'm walking home!'

But in the end I swapped with the wrangler and rode home on a mercifully placid mare.

Time moved on, and so did my girlfriends.

I've often thought that most of my happy relationships with girls seem to last three years. I spent three happy years with Nikki and soon my three years with Christine were up. We went our separate ways but it was quite a wrench. I was on tour at the time with a play called *Happy Birthday* by Mark Cameletti. This was a fun tour. There was Judy Carne, the knockabout girl from *Rowan and Martin's Laugh-in*, handsome, debonair Mark Burns, sexy Françoise Pascal and the lovely Sheila Ferris (wife of David Suchet).

Happy Birthday, like most farces, revolves around infidelity. I was playing Robert, a friend of Mark Burns, coming to stay for the weekend. Mark needed me because his mistress was due to arrive and he would pretend that she was my girlfriend. I made my first entrance carrying a suitcase and Mark would try to persuade me to stay. Eventually he shoves me and my suitcase bodily into the bedroom. After two pages I come out saying, 'I'm going.' Mark had to wrest the suitcase from my grip and fling it into the bedroom saying, 'Robert, you're staying!'

Every night the suitcase would be waiting for me in the wings and I would pick it up and walk on stage. One night I ambled out of my dressing-room casual and relaxed. I picked up the suitcase to make my entrance and nearly wrenched my arm out of the socket. I realised immediately that some very kind person had filled it with stage weights. I didn't have time to empty it – I could hear my cue. I staggered on stage and looked at Mark Burns. His eyes were twinkling with mischief.

'Robert, my dear fellow. How lovely to see you.'

You swine, I thought. *I'll get you for this!* I raised an eyebrow, lifted the suitcase and we carried on. I couldn't put the suitcase down because Mark had to chase me round the stage trying to persuade me to stay. It was getting heavier by the minute. Eventually he said, 'This is your bedroom and pushed me off stage.'

I opened the suitcase. It was absolutely full of stage weights. Judy Carne was standing there.

'Get your own back on him, leave them there,' she said. 'He has to throw that bag into the room in a minute.'

That was a good point. But I had a better idea. I took all the weights out and closed the case. Then when I came back on stage I pretended that it was still full. I hefted it in with a grunt and let it hang heavy on my arm. Mark looked at me. Realisation set in. *Oh no, I've got to pick that case up in a minute!*

I walked round the stage miming like mad. We came to the moment when he said, 'Robert, you're staying,' and he took the suitcase from me. He heaved at the thing with all his strength, but of course it was light as a feather. His momentum took him backwards like a tumbler. He took off, landed on the settee with the suitcase on top of him, where he burst out laughing. I corpsed as well. The audience were bewildered: why were these actors laughing? It may sound unprofessional, but playfulness and high jinks sometimes help to keep actors fresh and on their toes and in that show they were a reflection of the fun we were having working together.

So the show was fun. But my love life was not such comedy. I drove back from Eastbourne one night to find a cold and empty house with coat hangers clattering in the closets. Christine had walked out on me.

I had no idea why. I could not think of a reason. I thought we were great together. On the Sunday I rang some friends and found out where she was. She had moved in with another man. I drove round to the farmhouse where they lived and it dawned on me that this had been going on for some time behind my back.

By chance she was alone in the house. The chap she had moved in with was down in London on business. I confronted her and asked her why she had left me.

'I just can't stand you being away. I want my man to be with me all the time. I hate it that you're always touring.'

'I've got to make a living.'

We talked a long time and I told her that I loved her. She agreed to give it one more go and we took all her clothes back to my house. On Sunday night we talked about getting engaged.

'If that's what you want, we'll have a ring on your finger by next weekend. I'm down in London this week with the tour, but next week I'm back doing Harrogate, so we'll have the whole week to look for a ring.'

She kissed me goodbye on the Monday and I drove down to London. Judy Carne was the first person I saw.

'How'd it go with Christine?'

'Everything's fine. We're back together.' I felt like I had resolved the crisis.

I rang home. There was no reply. I rang again later. Still no reply. I got the dreaded phone call on Tuesday morning. A friend told me. 'She's gone back. Your house is empty.'

I was devastated. We had talked about marriage and everything. But in the end Christine couldn't deal with the lifestyle, with having me on tour. There are highs and lows in touring – the highs are the thrills of being on stage, the lows missing your loved one in the loneliness of your dressing room.

Another Christine, Christine McKenna, the lovely young star of *Flambards* for Yorkshire Television, flitted like a butterfly in and out of my life. That relationship didn't last long but we remained friends. So much so that one weekend found Christine and I with Clive Hornby and his girlfriend down at Joe Allen's, the well-known theatrical watering hole in the West End. Sitting two tables away were Diane Langton and Gemma Craven.

I had met Gemma years previously when she was engaged to Brian Marshall, a young comedian who was appearing in *Queenie's Castle* for Yorkshire Television with Diana Dors. He went on to do his own show called *Where's Brian?* and Gemma was one of the guests. Brian was doubling up at the time at the Batley Variety Club and I went along to keep Gemma company while he was on stage. So we knew each other even if we couldn't call each other friends.

I caught Gemma's eye and she looked strangely at me and turned away. I turned to Clive Hornby.

'There's Gemma Craven. I used to know her, but it looks like she's gone all Hollywood and superior now that she's starring in the West End.'

'Well, bugger it,' said Clive. 'Don't have that. If you want to go over and say hello, you go ahead.'

'She won't remember me,' I answered but I allowed myself to be persuaded. She was, after all, ravishingly pretty.

I took the bull by the horns and went over. Unknown to me, as our eyes had met, Gemma had turned to Diane Langton and said, 'There's Frazer Hines over there. I used to know him when I was engaged to Brian Marshall. But look, he obviously doesn't want to know me now, because I'm not with Brian anymore.'

I went over to her table.

'Hello Gemma. Do you remember me?'

'Yes of course. Frazer! How are you? Do sit down.'

So I sat down and we started to catch up.

'What are you doing right now?' I asked.

'I'm in a musical, *They're Playing our Song*.'

'Oh, that's right. I hear very good things about it.'

'Have you seen the show yet?'

'To be honest,' I said. 'It's not really my cup of tea. You know, American boy meets girl schmaltzy musical. I don't really fancy it.'

'Oh. I see.'

'But look, would you fancy having supper next weekend? I'll be down in London to do one of those Celebrity Superstars things where Lindsay de Paul and Michael Aspel fire bows and arrows and run relay races and play five-a-side football with Geoff Hurst. You know the sort of thing. We could meet then.'

'I'd love to,' said Gemma. 'But really you ought to come and see the show as well.'

Well, I thought, *if we're going to go out for supper I had better see the show after all.* So I went on the Friday and boy! She was good. In fact she was terrific and the show was excellent too. She and Tom Conti made a marvellous pair. (Also in the chorus, by the way, was a certain Deena Payne, who was wowing everybody as Viv Windsor in *Emmerdale*.)

We had supper on Friday. It was lovely and we made a date for Saturday. Gemma had a matinee and an evening show. And because I had Superstars we met up afterwards and went for supper again. Then we drove back to my hotel. We parked and I kissed her goodnight and she kissed me goodnight. So I kissed her again. And she kissed me again.

This was one of those times when the two voices in your head battle for ascendancy. The little devil said, 'Take her upstairs to your room – you're on to something here.' And the little angel was saying, 'No, no, no – this could be special. Take it slowly. Treat it with respect.' The little angel won and I watched her drive away, knowing that something had started.

Every weekend thereafter was the same. I would finish in the studio, then drive down and pick her up for supper. Sundays were spent driving to Southend and attending mass and lunches with her parents. Every weekend I was meeting more friends and relations. I felt as though I was being vetted.

I was also going out at the same time, with a lovely Yorkshire girl called Debbie. I was, as they say, torn between two lovers. But then I got an unexpected ultimatum.

One Sunday morning I was lying in bed and the phone went. It was my friend, Roger Lord.

'Have you seen the papers?' he asked.

'No Roger. I'm still in bed.'

'Well get yourself downstairs sharpish and have a look at them.'

'Why?'

'Your engagement is front-page news.'

I rushed downstairs. It was true!. *Frazer Hines, Gemma Craven to be married*. Damn! I know that if you're in the public eye you have to put up with this sort of thing but I don't have to like having my private life made public property like that. Still, it was done. I had to live with it now.

I looked out of my window and there were three or four photographers waiting for a quote. I didn't feel like talking about it. I went back upstairs where I still had Roger on 'hold'.

'You're right Rog. And what's more, the press are outside.'

'Be ready at your back door in five minutes,' said Roger. 'I'll honk the horn twice. You can come back to my place.'

I threw some clothes on and listened at my back door. Bang on time I heard Roger's car pull up and he honked his horn twice. I sped out of my little cottage and dived into the passenger seat.

'Go! Go! Go!'

Off he drove, tyres squealing.

'They're coming after us!' he said.

But they were on foot and we made a clean getaway. At Roger's house his wife Beryl was cooking Sunday lunch. Roger sat back with a drink in his hand and said, 'D'you know, Frazer. I've always wanted to do that.'

But I was gutted. My hand had been forced. Gemma had leaked our engagement to the press and, in 'Hines Sight', I should have taken that as a sign. She later pulled the same trick about our divorce.

During this time my dear friend and racehorse trainer, Steve Nesbitt, was desperately ill with cancer. I visited him at his stables, Kingsley House, in Middleham as often as I could. I went to see him one day and found the door ajar, so I went straight in. Myra, his wife, had brought his bed downstairs to the lounge.

'Hello, Frazer,' he croaked.

'Stevie, you don't look too well, lad.'

'I'm not too bad.' But his voice sounded like he was on death's door.

'Can I make you a cup of tea?'

'Aye, lad. Cup of tea would be nice.' While I was making it he said, 'Frazer, I don't think I'm long for this Earth.'

'Stevie, none of that sort of talk. I'm getting married in November. You're expected to attend.'

'Aye, I must try and hang on till then.'

'Hang on be blowed! You're going to see me married.'

I drove home that day with a heavy heart. I was sure I was going to lose my friend very soon and I didn't expect to see him at the wedding.'

Two days later I popped back to Middleham to see Steve again. I rang the doorbell. The door opened and there was Steve, up and about.

'Frazer! How are you doing?'

'Steve, you're up.'

'Aye, I feel much better. Come and have a cup of tea.'

I couldn't believe it. I had brought Steve a funny book on horse-racing. I read a passage out of it aloud.

'Don't!' he said, coughing. 'Don't make me laugh, you little bastard, you know it hurts when I laugh!'

Well, I left that day in much higher spirits. It looked like Steve was in remission and he would be coming to the wedding after all. About three days later I went to ride out at Steve's. Afterwards I took the saddle off Excavator Lady and walked in to Steve's house and there he was again, flat out in bed in the lounge.

'Steve, what's the matter?'

'Oh, Frazer, I'm not well again today.'

'You were fine the other day.'

It was very hard to come to terms with. Every few days Steve would be up and about and you could believe that he'd not only be at the wedding but leading the revelry. Then he'd relapse and be back in bed.

The next time I was there Steve was in good shape again. 'Oh, I feel much better again, Frazer.'

'Steve,' I said. 'Will you do me a favour? Are you coming or going?'

'How do you mean?'

'Me and the stable lads have had your coffin up and down that long drive five times in the last fortnight. And it's bloody heavy. Are you dying or stopping?'

He collapsed on the floor, helpless with mirth. 'You little bastard! How dare you! I'll tell you how it's going to go. I'm going to hang on to see you married, you little bugger.'

And bless him, hang on he did. He and Myra came all the way down to Westcliffe-on-Sea to see us married.

A lot of nonsense has been printed by the papers about my being late for the wedding – acceptable for a woman but not a man of course – and how my ex-wife had wished I hadn't turned up at all. Let me put the record straight. Yes, I was late – along with my best man, my agent Al Mitchell, the Krankies and about a dozen other cars following me to Westcliffe. We were all stuck in a freak snow-storm which totally blocked the roads. We had left an hour early with every intention of stopping for a little 'Dutch Courage' just outside of Westcliffe. Lucky we did or we'd have been even later. As we were crawling along I said to Al, 'A phone box, I'll ring her (there were no mobile phones in those days), and we pulled over and I dialled Gemma's number.

Gemma's father answered, 'Oh, it's Frazer, you are what?' He turned to Gemma who was about to cry. 'No, no don't worry, he's turning up, he's just stuck in a traffic jam, it's the snow.'

I put the phone down as Mustapha bounded across: 'Quick Frazer, I've bought a motorbike – we can drive down the outside of the traffic and get there.'

'Musti,' I said. 'We are all in top hat and tails, they'll get ruined – a nice idea though.'

He looked disappointed. His James Bond fantasy out of the window.

After the wedding, of course, I took Gemma on honeymoon. She didn't know where we were going. I kept it a secret. We drove to Tilbury where we found a ship called the *Zazakstan*, our honeymoon cruise vessel.

'It's a Russian ship!' said Gemma.

'Yes …'

'Russian food's awful. I've been there and I don't like the food.'

'It'll be English food,' I reassured her and she agreed to board the ship, although looking like a child who was being sent to bed without any supper.

We were feted on that ship. Our bags were carried up the gangplank. I had booked a huge suite right at the front of the ship, with a lovely lounge, bedroom and bathroom. Waiting for us on the table were two bottles of champagne in a bucket of ice and a card which read, 'Welcome Mr and Mrs Hines; the Captain and crew of CTC liners.'

I for one enjoyed that honeymoon. The ship went to Rotterdam, Lisbon, down to Tangiers, Tenerife and Madeira. Although we were on honeymoon we made a lot of friends and acquaintances.

The ship's purser was a little man called Victor who wore literally rose-tinted spectacles. We struck up a bond with him. Nothing was too much trouble. We were treated like royalty, but I think that our room was bugged. Why would I think that? I will tell you. I turned to Gemma one day and said, 'I've lost a button on my shirt. I must ask one of the maids to sew it back.'

We then went off to amuse ourselves for the day and when we came back to the cabin I remembered my shirt. I was about to take it to the maid when I noticed that the button had been replaced. So was the room bugged? Well, the Cold War was on. But it is hard to imagine what sort of intelligence the KGB expected to gather from a honeymooning couple!

One night there was lobster on the menu. There was a buffet and everybody queued up. But the people at the front of the queue were taking two or three lobsters each and by the time we got to the table there were no more lobsters. We just had Russian salad, Hungarian goulash and Polish sausage.

'Look, Gemma,' I said. 'A Warsaw Pact Lunch!'

The next morning Victor wanted to be congratulated on his lobster.

'Mr Hines, you haff goot lobster last night.'

'No, we didn't.'

'You did not enjoy lobster?'

'We didn't get any.'

'Yes – we plenty lobster for the whole passenger.'

'I'm afraid a very decadent greed overcame the people in front of us in the queue. Some people were taking three or four lobsters and there were none left by the time we got there.'

'I see. Today you haff lunch in your cabin. Twelve o'clock.'

'Well, there's really no need …'

'You go. Cabin. Twelve o'clock.' Victor insisted.

So twelve o'clock. We go. And there, beautifully presented, were four lobsters and two bottles of champagne, courtesy of Victor: 'Everybody must have lobster on ship.'

On New Year's Eve 1981, we were sitting off the coast of Madeira where a magnificent firework display welcomed in the New Year. Gemma and I and a Scots fellow were watching it, warming ourselves against the chilly night with a bottle of Chivas Regal. At the stroke of midnight the figures 1981 were lit up in fireworks and then the *one* turned into a *two*. It was 1982 and we all cheered. It was a lovely romantic night.

The cruise ship docked at Tilbury and I drove back to Yorkshire with my new bride. Almost the moment we got in I received the phone call I was dreading. It was Steve Nesbitt's daughter, Carol Moore.

'My dad died while you were on honeymoon.'

I know it's irrational but I can't shake the feeling that maybe if I hadn't got married Steve would still be with us. I always felt he was hanging on to see 'the little bugger' married. Steve was the best friend a man could have and I still miss him.

Tony Palmer had cast Gemma in his 1983 TV film series *Wagner*, starring Richard Burton. She was due to start filming about two days after we got back from our honeymoon. We quickly unpacked all our honeymoon cruising clothes, packed up a fresh set of gear and headed straight off again to Austria and Switzerland.

Her first day on the set an assistant came over and said, 'Gemma – Mr Burton would like to meet you.'

So she went to his caravan. And two minutes later she came out again, 'Darling, Richard wants to meet you.'

I went all cold all over. Even after my years in show-business and even after all the great stars I had worked with, this was still something special. Richard Burton was practically the definition of a film star. A little awestruck I went to his caravan … and you couldn't hope to meet a nicer man.

'Well now, Mr and Mrs Hines is it?' He said in that magnificent, rich Welsh baritone of his. 'Sit down and I'll make a cup of tea. Milk and sugar?'

'Uh … Yeah…' I couldn't believe it. Richard Burton making me a cup of tea.

'Now then, Gemma. We're going to have a good time with this picture. Frazer, you're an actor as well, aren't you?'

'Did Gemma tell you?'

'No, I found that out myself,' he smiled. He had obviously done his homework. He had found out all about Gemma, including who her husband was and what he did for a living.

'This *Emmerdale Farm* thing – where's it set? Somerset? What sort of an accent do you have to have? Terribly "oo-ar", is it?'

'No, it's Yorkshire – it's in a Yorkshire accent.'

And so we talked about a tin-pot TV show with perhaps the world's leading man. After tea Burton was called on set. 'See you all tomorrow.'

'What a nice man,' I said to Gemma.

Gemma was called to the set the next day, so I stayed back at the hotel and then went for a wander around Vienna. The second day she came back to announce that Richard wanted to have dinner with us that night. Marvellous. That would be lovely – a big dinner with Burton and his friends and cronies.

We had to be downstairs in the hotel lobby at 8 o'clock and we were there promptly in our best bibs and tuckers. Richard's assistant came and ushered us into the dining room where there was a small table set for just four. The dinner was to be with just Richard, his assistant, Gemma and me.

Richard regaled us over dinner with cricketing stories because he was a great cricket fan and I told him tales of playing cricket with Fred Truman.

Richard became animated. 'You've played with Fred Truman? Has he bowled against you?'

'Well now, I think so.'

'You *think* so? How's that?'

'I didn't actually *see* the ball.'

I was very sad when I heard of Richard Burton's death. There was no side to the man. Imagine a man like that, as big a film star as the world had seen, happy to spend his time gossiping with a soap-opera actor.

The *Wagner* shoot came to an end and we returned home. With Gemma away a lot and not being a cook, I used to eat out. In the end I thought, *if I'm eating out, why don't I eat at my own place?* I decided to open a restaurant called Frazer's – an American-style diner. I couldn't do it alone so two waiters I knew from a couple of restaurants I'd frequented got talking and said they would join the venture, but it was not quite what I envisaged. I was out-voted on the style of the restaurant and Peppermint Place was born, a huge chrome and glass modern pizzeria, with a white piano as the centrepiece. I didn't much mind, I was going to be Humphrey Bogart, sitting at the number one table with a cigar!

We opened in Horsforth, much to Gemma's annoyance. She wasn't keen on the idea, but turned up on the opening night with her glittery jacket and welcomed everybody as the host's wife.

If you're running a restaurant you have to be there every night, counting money or working the till, or your wife has to be there. You just need to be on top of it. After about eighteen months the writing was on the wall and Peppermint Place closed down.

Now, whenever we went out to eat I would pick up the bill, as a traditional husband. But Gemma was a West End star and was earning four or five times what I was making in *Emmerdale Farm*. One day I decided to get even with her. Roger Lord, Gemma and I went to a Greek restaurant in the centre of Leeds, where they also had Greek dancing. The bill came and I said, 'Your turn, Gemma. Why don't you treat us for once?'

'No, you're my husband. You ought to pay.'

'So I said, 'Roger, have you ever tried Greek dancing?'

'No, Frazer.'

'Let's try this one.'

So I got Roger up and started showing him some Greek steps, a kind of Zorba dance. The bouzouki music got faster and faster and I manoeuvred him towards the door. As we got to the front door with our legs kicking the air, I said, 'Bye Gemma, thanks for lunch,' and Roger and I danced out the door and did a runner for the car-park. That was one time that Gemma actually paid for us.

On reflection we only had one proper row when we were married and even then it was her 'Don't you realise who I am?' attitude that caused the trouble. We went for a Sunday lunch at Napoleon's Casino in Bradford and after lunch we started to play a little on the tables.

There's a big sign there saying, 'Please do not take photographs'. Gemma, of course, got a camera out and took a snapshot of Lillian and Gabriel, her parents and of me against the table. A manager came over to me and said, 'Mr Hines, please would you tell your wife there are no photographs permitted.'

'I've already told her.'

'Would you mind telling her again?'

So I went to Gemma and told her again: no photographs.

'Who told you that?' She demanded.

'Well, the manager.'

'He can tell me himself, can't he?'

'He's come to me.'

'Why's he come to you?'

'Because I'm the member of the club and I'm your husband.'

'Doesn't he know who I am? Let him come to me. If he doesn't want me to take pictures, he can come and tell me.'

We had a few words and went out to the car-park.

'Look, you should have stopped taking the pictures,' I said.

'Well, if he isn't man enough to tell me to my face …'

'Gemma, I'm telling you. You should not have taken photographs.'

She looked at me and curled her lip. 'You're just jealous because I've worked with Richard Burton,' she said, turning on her heel.

I saw red. I kicked her, I am ashamed to say, right up the bottom. She turned around, eyes blazing, and raised her fist to me. An Irish voice behind me said, 'You know Frazer, oi should have done that moiself, years ago.' It was Gabriel, Gemma's father. She gave him a murderous look, turned away and stalked off.

Gemma had some filming to do one weekend, so I thought, *Good I can ride to Newmarket Town Plate* – a famous horse race.

I rang round some trainers for a ride in the race and I finally got an offer from Jim Ratcliffe.

'I've got a nice horse for you, Frazer, called My Boy Too. He'll give you a good ride. I'm also trying to sell him, so see if you can make a good showing for me.'

'I'll do my best,' I packed my bags and went down to Newmarket.

There was a phone call on Saturday night. It was Gemma. 'Hello, darling,' I said.

'Where are you?' I knew immediately that she was not best pleased. Her voice was frosted with her annoyance.

'I'm in Newmarket.'

'What are you doing in Newmarket?'

'I'm riding tomorrow.'

'Well I want you home.'

'But you're away filming.'

'No I'm not. I came home early.'

'That's lovely, but I can't just come home right now.'

'But I want you.'

'I'm sorry darling. But I can't let these people down, I'm jocked up.'

'Look, you're an actor not a jockey. Come home now.'

'You don't understand, I'm the jockey for the horse. I have to be there tomorrow.'

'I hope you fall off,' and with that she hung up.

I rode the horse and we finished fifth or sixth. The Newmarket Town Plate is three and three-quarter miles. It's a long race and it felt good to be riding My Boy Too. I drove home elated because that wasn't a bad position. I had done pretty well for Jim Ratcliffe and I thought I'd done pretty well for me too.

Mark Pitman, son of Grand National winning trainer Jenny, was having his first ride on a horse called Arctic Prince.

'If you follow me round,' I said, 'you'll win this.'

He didn't. And he didn't. We still laugh about it when we meet up though. And after all, Mark did go on to ride the winner of the *Cheltenham Gold Cup*.

It does seem that whenever I'm on a high there is always a hammer blow waiting round the next corner. My mother called me to tell me that my middle brother, Roy, was very ill with cancer. I was supposed to be filming that week. I called YTV and said 'I have to go to London tomorrow. My brother's very ill and he wants to see me.' But they insisted that the schedules were too tight.

For a week I couldn't get down and Roy was desperate to see me. He had read that if you drank holy water from Lourdes it would give you strength to fight the disease. Gemma's Uncle Paddy was a priest and he got hold of some holy water for me. Gemma took it to Roy in the hospital.

The press called me, 'I hear your brother's dying of cancer.'

'No, he's very ill with cancer.'

'And you're coming down tomorrow, aren't you?'

'Yes, I've finally managed to get a day off. I'll be there.'

'What train are you getting? We'll meet you for a photograph.'

'Hang on,' I said. 'I'm not coming for that. It's not a publicity stunt. I'm coming to see my brother.'

'Yeah, it'll be a great picture – Frazer Hines in Mercy Dash to Dying Brother.'

'You're not listening. My brother is ill with cancer – he's not dying. He's fighting it all the way. Now, please, no pictures. Let me just go and visit Roy in peace, OK?'

I went the next day and Alan Whitehead turned up and went with me. We tried to cheer Roy up with chat and stories. I mentioned that I had just been to Arizona with Gemma for a *TV Times* shoot. As a great lover of old western riding he asked if I had brought back any souvenirs.

'Yes. I've brought you back a lovely belt-buckle. I forgot to bring it though – I'll bring it next time I visit.' I've still got it.

All too soon it was time to leave. I got on the train to go back home having seen my once-fit brother lying wracked in pain in a hospital bed finding even speech difficult. You can imagine how I was feeling at that point.

The next day the papers ran the story: 'Frazer Hines Dashes to Bring Holy Water to Dying Brother.' I was livid. I wanted to kill somebody.

And within a day Roy had gone.

My mother called me to tell me that my brother had died. I phoned the newspaper reporter and called him every name under the sun.

'You're a murderer!' I said. 'You killed my brother!'

'He was dying anyway.'

'What? He was fighting for his life and then he reads in the paper that he's dying of cancer. He must have thought, oh that's it then. It's all over for me. I'm actually dying of cancer. Nobody's told me. I might as well just stop fighting. You killed my brother.'

Is there anything in this? I felt at the time that Roy was fighting all the way and he was a strong lad, our Roy. If he hadn't read in the newspaper that the game was up, I think he might have pulled through and still been with us.

Things like that were wearing me down. I was missing my wife and following a punishing schedule. I was driving two hundred miles every Friday night down that miserable one-way street M1 after work. I would collect Gemma, who was on a high having just come off stage and would want to be taken out to the Caprice or somewhere similar to burn off the adrenaline. I had just completed a week of heavy studio filming and I was tired and wanted to go home and enjoy being a husband.

All this weighed on my mind and I felt it weighed on our relationship. In the end, to help our marriage, I decided to leave *Emmerdale Farm*.

Chapter Eight
1984

George Orwell was right: 1984 was a bad year. All right, unlike Winston Smith in the book, I didn't have rats gnawing at my brain, but I did have the press snapping at my heels most of the time I spent up in Pitlochry in Scotland, and there are times when it's hard to tell the difference.

It was a year I would not want to live through again. Every day is etched in my memory. And yet it started out so well. My marriage appeared in shape. The offers were coming in and when I had left *Emmerdale Farm* I had received a lovely letter from Yorkshire Television's executive producer and head of drama, David Cunliffe, one of the last great men of television. He said that he was sorry I was leaving, but he understood why, and he thanked me for all the hard work I had put into the early years of *Emmerdale Farm*. He finished up, 'If you ever want to return, Frazer, I'm sure the door will always be open.' To cap it all, my horse Excavator Lady won at Wetherby on 10 January.

Looking back I realise there were bad signs which I should have noticed earlier and like everybody else I have regrets. Mostly about Gemma. The worst of our failings, Gemma and I, was that we were lacking in the communication department. I like to think I know a little better now, but however much I was to blame for inadequate communication back then, there was no excuse for the thoughtless way in which Gemma chose to end our marriage.

I believe that I was trying to make a success of it.

Gemma and I had bought a horse together called Escapism. It was my way of trying to involve her, not only in my new hobby, but also in an important part of my life. Gemma seemed to enjoy going to the race meetings and certainly got excited when our boy was due to run. And of course, she looked marvellous at the races; we had great fun dressing up for them together. It was champagne all the way at the track and with the horse, and she seemed to get on well with my racing friends. Although there were times when I wondered if she genuinely liked them, or whether she just pretended to for my sake. Escapism did well for us, winning and getting placed, and to be honest if you've got a horse that is paying for itself, you should count it a success. He won a big race at Doncaster and very soon afterward we had a phone call asking if we would sell Escapism, offering a fair price. In fact, we would have come out of the deal ahead. I was tempted, but Gemma dug her heels in.

'No way, Fraz. We're not selling him. He's our first horse together and I don't care how much they're offering, he's not for sale.'

There's an old racing saying that your first profit is always the best one – or to put it another way, take the money and run. Sure enough, a fortnight later Escapism took a nasty knock and hurt a tendon. That was it. He wouldn't run again. In the end we luckily managed to get a good price for him and he was off to Wales with his new owner, Graham Lloyd, to start a new life as a stallion. Looking back, I might have envied him. I know many a man with a sore foot who would love to be put to stud.

Two days later Gemma and I went to a Barnsley Junior Chamber of Commerce Personality Dinner where I was nominated for Yorkshire Man of the Year: it's quite an exciting prospect to know that your whole county has been voting for you to win what is a coveted award in that part of the world. I came second to that very nice Geoffrey Smith, the TV and radio gardener. I gave my speech and collected my runners-up tankard and sat down. My wife was less pleased than I was. In fact, she had a mouth like a torn zip. She liked winners!

'Don't worry,' I said. 'I wasn't off,' (a racing term for non-triers) and we enjoyed the rest of the evening.

On Sunday I went alone to Harrogate where my mother had just moved into a nursing home. It had come to the time when I wasn't able to be there enough to care for her, and to be honest I'm not brilliant at things like that anyway. Also, I had my marriage to think about. I discussed it with my mum and she was happy enough to go into the wonderful home we found for her. So that was my destination while Gemma flew off to Dublin. In the evening I did a show for BBC Leeds called *On Your Way*. I had no idea that very shortly my wife would be saying that to me.

On 2 February I went to London to rehearse my second appearance on *3-2-1*. The first time I had played a debonair, handsome Mississippi gambler. This time, I was to play … a fox! Yes, a fox – as in a small dog-like furry number. I made a mental note: *Frazer, next time* read *the script before accepting the part*. Mind you, we were all in the same boat. We were doing *Aesop's Fables*. Frank Thornton, best known as Captain Peacock in *Are You Being Served?*, was a tortoise, Anna Dawson was a blackbird and Tyler Butterworth (talented son of comedienne Janet Brown and actor Peter Butterworth) was a hare. We recorded all the songs in London and rehearsed the show, then came back to Leeds to record the finished article at Yorkshire Television's studios. Gemma sat with my screen mother Sheila Mercier in the audience and during filming breaks I had them both tickle my furry fox's tum.

I had no inkling of the cataclysm that was to come.

On Monday, the day before Valentine's day, Gemma began rehearsals for *Loot*. Though I wasn't aware of it at the time that was the beginning of the end. On Valentine's Day itself I drove up to Sedgefield where Excavator Lady was running. She ran badly. Now, it's always a short journey home when your horse has won, but a really long one when it has lost.

Back in London I went alone to the AGM of the Amateur Riders Association of Great Britain. It has always been very important to me to keep alive the true spirit of amateur riding here in England. In the evening, Gemma had learnt enough of her lines so we could afford to go out to see Victoria Wood on stage, who was brilliant, as she always is.

I was booked to play in rep up in Pitlochry for the summer season, so I phoned Sue Wilson, our director, to see if she could find a little cottage for me to rent. I was thinking of something cosy and homely where Gemma could come and visit me whenever she could get away. How romantic. How misconceived.

I drove up to Pitlochry with three friends, horse trainer Richard Whitaker, David Button and Raymond Shuttleworth. We made it a bit of a golfing weekend, staying at Gleneagles on the way.

The place Sue found for me was the most delightful little cottage, owned by one of the directors of the theatre. It was surrounded by pine trees and there was a little babbling brook, with a deer on the lawn. I was looking forward to my stay in Pitlochry.

I was back in London in time for Gemma's preview of *Loot* on Wednesday. It was a really good show. She was excellent in it as was Leonard Rossiter and the rest of the cast.

It was back up to Doncaster on the Saturday for me, where Excavator Lady ran fourth, ridden by Phil Tuck. I had began to know every filling station and every exit on the M1.

The weekend saw me back for a big Sunday lunch with my wife. I gave her a massage in preparation for her opening night on the Tuesday. I was thrilled for her in her success and we celebrated in high spirits after the show with the rest of the cast. Nobody at the opening-night party would have guessed that there was anything wrong between us. Including me.

Wednesday was a sad day for me. I kissed Gemma goodbye and got into my car, at this time a red Mercedes 280SE, and I drove to Yorkshire where I was to swap it for a newer model – another Merc, but a gold one this time. This new car had only done 7,000 miles. By the end of Pitlochry the milometer showed a rather higher figure!

I arrived at Pitlochry, unpacked the car, filled the fridge and rang Gemma. There was no reply. *Well she's still on stage*, I thought. *I'll call her later.*

When I called the theatre later she had gone out for supper. *She'll probably call me.*

But she didn't. I spent two days trying to get hold of her, and got no reply, but, I thought, when you're rehearsing during the day and playing at night you're apt to be busy and tired.

On Monday 19 March we read-through *On the Razzle* in Pitlochry. This is a very funny play by Tom Stoppard and I was playing the part of Weinberl.

It's about two shop-workers who go out 'on the razzle' one night in Vienna.

I was still trying to get in touch with Gemma and I finally managed to get hold of her on the Thursday.

'Gemma, where are you?'

'I've been rehearsing the play. Trying to get it right.' She sounded ratty.

'Look, I've got some news. You know we thought I was away for at least six weeks to rehearse and everything. Well, the weekend after next, I'm not working at all. We've all got the weekend off. And I'm coming home.'

'Oh,' she said. 'When?'

'Well, I'll come home on the late Friday coach and I'll be with you all day Saturday and Sunday.'

'I see. When do you go back?'

'I'll go back on the Monday and then …' An alarm bell rang in my head. Hang on: she's not over the moon. It's not, 'It'll be great to see you,' its 'When are you leaving?'

'Is anything wrong?' I asked.

'No, it's just that I might be working that weekend.'

'Doing what?'

'I'm doing the play on Saturday and I'm doing a commercial on Sunday.'

'Well that's all right,' I said. 'I'll come down anyway. I could see the play.'

'But you've seen it already.'

'I'll see it again. Or I'll wait at home for you. And I'll come on Sunday and watch you make the commercial.'

'You don't really want to do that. Look, you don't really have to come home, do you?' she asked.

'You don't want me to come home, do you?'

'Oh don't be silly. Of course you can come if you want to.'

We ended the phone call. I knew something was up. Every time we spoke after that, the conversations were undercut with a feeling of foreboding. But maybe it's the play, I thought. It can do funny things to you, immersing yourself into a part to get it right. I put it out of my mind. I still thought it was going to be a good year. As if to confirm my uncertain feelings, on

Grand National day in 1984 I backed the first four finishers!'

That weekend I picked Gemma up after the show on Saturday and suggested that the next day we go out for Sunday lunch.

'No, I'll cook for you,' she said.

She prepared roast lamb and we had a lovely meal. Then she came out with it.

'Frazer, I'm leaving you.'

Well that was out of the blue. I had worked out that there was a problem of some kind but I had no idea it was of this magnitude. I was stunned. 'Why?'

'I've just fallen out of love with you.'

I spent the rest of the day asking, 'Why?' but that was the only answer she had. I wondered if it was just a phase … the strain of the new play … I didn't know. She told me she was going to Jersey to do a weekend show, I said I'd join her there. But she refused.

On Monday morning I had no choice. I had to go back to Scotland to open *On the Razzle*. On the opening night, there was a card from Gemma. 'Wishing you luck. All my love, your wife,' *Frazer*, I thought, *your worries are over*. It was just a phase she was going through.

The show went really well. We were a great company, John Webb, Phillip Reader, Sunnie and Annie Tobin. *On the Razzle* just got better and better.

Once that show was up and running we had to start rehearsing *Hedda Gabler* by Henrik Ibsen during the day. In this I was playing Ejlert Løvborg, a writer who was in love with Hedda Gabler.

Gemma was coming up to Leeds on the Sunday, but I couldn't get down because of performances and rehearsals. I didn't know then that the purpose of her trip was to move her possessions out of the marital home.

There are many things you can forgive a person for but there is one thing I can never forgive Gemma for. Her timing could hardly have been worse. Especially since she lives in the world of show-business, as I do and she knew the score.

It was the first night of *Hedda Gabler*, which is a very intense play.

The cast are always wound up on opening night and in *Hedda* there is little to lighten their mood. Now, my reaction to the nerves is not to pace up and down or bite my fingernails. I lie down and sleep on the floor. I've always done that. It's my way of dealing with it. So there I was, asleep on the floor, half an hour before curtain up and the phone rang. Somebody called me: 'Frazer, it's your wife.' I leapt up and dashed to the phone, expecting to hear her say, 'Good luck, darling.'

But she wasn't even thinking of me. Her voice was businesslike. 'Hello, Frazer. Look, I've had a press conference today. About you and me breaking up. I thought I ought to tell you that it will be in the papers tomorrow.'

'What? Why?'

'I think it's better out in the open.'

I was horrified. I couldn't think. Curtain up was only minutes away.

'But why call a press conference? If it really is over, why not let it just fade out. If people are going to have to know, let them read it between the stop press and the racing results on the back page of the *Evening Standard*. Why does it have to be headlines?'

But no, Gemma had to go and call a press conference. And inform me five minutes before a performance. I don't know how I got through the show that night.

I was meant to play football for the Showbiz Eleven at Glenrothes just down the road that Sunday. I rang Jess Conrad and cancelled. My heart wasn't in entertaining people.

The news broke. The headline: Gemma Craven leaves husband Frazer Hines. Within three days Pitlochry was besieged by the press hounds looking for me. The only papers who were not baying for a statement from me were the *Daily Worker* and the *Sporting Life*.

My friend and business manager, Carl Gresham and his partner Helen, drove through the night to keep the hounds at bay. They had been round to most of the cast's houses to ask them where I was, but they had closed ranks and wouldn't say. Somebody in the village of Pitlochry, most probably quite innocently, pointed out my cottage. And from then on, every morning at half past eight there was knocking on the door.

'Frazer, we know you are in there. Can we have a word?'

I remember Carl going downstairs and standing at the door, saying, 'Mr Hines says his private life is private. He won't say anything.'

'Can he come and tell us himself?'

'No.'

'Can we just get one quote?'

'No.'

'Well, could Mr Hines just come and tell us to piss off?'

Carl said, 'Mr Hines does not use that kind of language. So the answer is still no. Goodbye.'

I got a call from Roy, the company manager at the theatre.

'Frazer, they're all around the theatre, the stage door, everywhere. You had better not drive in. I'll come and get you.'

When Roy came over, I got in the boot of his car to be driven to the theatre. Round the back and in through the fire exit. At the end of the show, when I might have been in the bar, laughing and joking with the rest of the cast, I was out the fire exit, into the boot of Roy's car and back to my lonely little beseiged cottage. And that was my life for the next three or four weeks until the press got bored of my silence and left.

The following week I had a call from Gemma. The coast was clear so she was coming to Pitlochry to see me. My heart, which had been in turmoil for the past fortnight, sailed into calmer waters. She would be on flight BD247, she said. I couldn't wait.

I drove to the airport and met the plane. She wasn't on it.

I phoned her. She had finished *Loot* so I called at 7pm. She wasn't in. She finally answered my calls at 2am.

'What the hell are you ringing me at this time for?'

'I've been trying to get you all night. You were supposed to be flying up today.'

'Oh that,' she said. 'I didn't catch the plane.'

'I know you didn't catch the bloody plane! I went to meet it.'

'Well relax. What are you worrying for? I'll be on tomorrow's flight.'

I drove again to Edinburgh. The plane landed and the passengers began to disembark. Gemma wasn't there. I thought, not again! Finally, when the plane was otherwise empty, she emerged, the last passenger off. I still think she did that on purpose to wind me up. But at least she had turned up this time. Perhaps now we could talk things through. My sense of relief was short-lived. She reached the arrivals gate and there she was, Grumpy Craven, face like thunder.

I reached out to welcome her, but she walked past me coldly saying, 'Hello.' And her only other words of greeting were when I was putting her bag in the boot of my new car. 'Nice car,' she said.

We drove to Pitlochry more or less in silence. The day outside the car was warm and sunny, but inside the car it was a fridge. I tried to lighten the mood with small-talk.

'The filly runs on Wednesday at Ripon,' I said. 'She's looking really well.' (We had bought another horse called Here We Go Again after we sold Escapism.)

'I won't be there.'

'But I thought you were staying for a fortnight. I've got the weekend off, and on Wednesday the filly's running …'

'I'll be going home on Sunday afternoon, after lunch with Richard and Liz.'

'But I thought you'd come to see me, I thought you'd be here for a while …'

'Frazer. We're having lunch with the Whitakers. I'm paying my training bill. And then I'm going.'

I dropped her off at the cottage and went to the theatre to play *On the Razzle*. When I got home that night she had made supper for us. You would think nothing had happened. We even lay together in the same bed.

'So how long is this trial separation to go on for?' I asked. 'Will we be like Chris Evert and John Lloyd? Will we be back together soon …?'

'Chris Evert and John Lloyd have got nothing to do with it. It's not a trial separation. I've left you.'

We had breakfast together on Saturday and she came to the matinee of *Razzle*. Between shows she came backstage. 'You were quite good. I enjoyed it.'

'Really?' It was the first pleasant thing she'd said to me all weekend.

'Yes, you were quite good.'

As I've said, by this time the press had drifted off and Gemma was able to come to the shows without being bothered. She only saw the first act of *Hedda Gabler*, though. After that she went into the bar with another cast member, Clare Rimmer, who wasn't in *Hedda* and they got quietly ratted together.

In the interval I had a phone call from the Krankies, who had been reading the papers. Janette was heartbroken. 'How could she leave you, Frazer?'

'You tell me. I've done nothing wrong. I haven't hit her. I haven't got drunk, or stolen her money. I've done none of the things a woman usually leaves a man for. I haven't slept with her best friend, nothing.'

Clare came to me after the show and said, 'She's waiting for you in the bar, Frazer. I've had a long talk with her. Yes, it might be over, but there's a chance it isn't.' My heart leapt again. It was a roller-coaster ride.

We drove to Leeds and on the Sunday we had lunch with Richard and Liz Whitaker. They too tried to persuade her to stay and see the filly run, but she insisted on leaving on the 4 o'clock train.

I took her to the station and found her a compartment. 'Are you sure you won't change your mind?'

'No.'

Her face was like stone.

'But I love you Gemma,' I cried.

'It's too late for that,' she answered impassively.

I got off the train and watched her face as it left the station. She showed no emotion as she stared back at me.

Tears welled up in my eyes and rolled down my cheeks.

Richard and Liz wanted me to stay with them for a while, 'The last thing you want is to go back to an empty house,' they said.

So I stayed with Richard *and* rode out because George Moore who had trained Excavator Lady from a two year old foal had entered her at Redcar the following Tuesday.

She ran really well in that race and finished third at 33 to 1. She had about 11 stone on her, but my weight had dropped to 10 stone. That was the good thing about Gemma leaving me. She left me in the flat season. So my weight came down and I had a nice big saddle. Thanks Gemma! Thanks a lot!

Jean Rogers rang to ask whether she and Toke Townley could come up and see me. Wonderful, I thought, I'll see some of the old gang. They arrived on Friday night and the next day we were playing *Hedda* for the matinee and *Razzle* in the evening. I got Jean, Justine, her beautiful young daughter, and Toke their tickets.

Hedda Gabler was going really well. I had made my last exit and was in the dressing-room feeling very low. Roy our company manager, brought the *Daily Star* in. The front page was a photograph of Gemma with a glass of wine in her hand at her front door. She had tears in her eyes.

'I still love him, but it won't work,' she was wailing to the press.

I looked at Roy.

'I don't understand Roy. I'm stuck up here in Scotland. I love her so deeply. She's down in London telling them she loves me too. We're two grown-up people. Why aren't we together? Why are we torturing each other?'

'Frazer, I just don't know.'

Roy went back to work, leaving me in the room with the photograph and my shattered feelings.

'Mr Hines. Stand by for curtain call.'

My head was in a whirl. I staggered up the stairs, heard the play finish, heard the applause. Walked on to the stage and took my first bow. I straightened up, and went for my second bow. Folks, I didn't come back up. I just kept on going and hit the stage with an almighty thump.

The cast all rallied round. It was like a Victorian tableau.

The audience applauded wildly. They thought it was part of the act. There was Løvborg, dead again at Hedda Gabler's feet.

But there, in amidst the applause, sounding like a distant public address tannoy, I could hear one voice, the voice of Annie Tobin, one of the actresses in the play.

'No, he really has collapsed. Is there a doctor in the house?'

They picked me up and laid me on the settee on stage. At Pitlochry there were no curtains, just blackout as you bow.

This man came on and held my hand.

'Don't worry,' he said.

'Are you a doctor?' I asked.

'In a way. I'm a psychiatrist.'

I sat bolt upright with tears running down my face. 'I don't need a psychiatrist. I just need my wife back.'

I looked up and there were Jean and Justine looking at me with great concern on their faces. I felt so embarrassed. I was crying like a baby.

Toke, Jean and Justine took me back to the hotel where I slept on Jean's bed for three hours. They woke me up with a cup of tea and took me back to the theatre where I had an evening performance of *On the Razzle*. I gave the performance of my life: for Jean and Justine and Toke.

It came to the curtain call. As I stepped forward to take my bow, I felt a hand on my waistcoat. I looked round and it was Phillip Reader who was playing Herr Zangler.

'Just in case you don't come up,' he mouthed.

But I took my bows and everybody clapped me on the back to congratulate me.

'Well done, Frazer. You were smashing.'

And Phillip said, 'You were great. Really wonderful. It was the performance of your life, Frazer. But I have to tell you this. On stage, your eyes were dead.'

With Gemma appearing in the papers again the press hounds returned in force. It was the same old scenario: the hounding, the baying for a statement, the hammering on the door at 8 o'clock in the morning.

Eventually Roy stepped forward and said, 'There's a young lady from the *Yorkshire Evening Post*. She says you know her. Can she be the spokesperson, so that you can give her the interview and she'll go back and give your side of the story to the rest of them.'

I remembered the name of the reporter from when I left *Emmerdale Farm*. She had come to Grange Park where we were filming, to do a piece on me and why I was leaving the programme. I had made her welcome, taken her into the caravan, given her coffee and talked freely with her.

The article came out: Frazer Hines bounded up to me like a young puppy wanting to be loved. He opened his caravan door and poured coffee down me like it was going out of fashion ... he even had the temerity to compare himself with the great actor Roger Moore ...'

Well yes. What I actually said was that, like Roger Moore, I enjoy a cigar after a meal. It was silly sensationalism. This young reporter obviously wanted to make a name for herself and she tore this interview apart.

So I thought a moment and then said to Roy, 'Yes, I'll see her. Tell her to meet me in the bar after the show and I'll speak to her and her alone.'

After the show I was able to go to the bar for once to drink with all the gang without being hounded by the press.

The girl came in. 'Hello, Frazer. Do you remember me?'

The room went quiet as I turned to look at her.

'Yes I do. You're the girl I tried to make welcome at Grange Park on my last day on *Emmerdale Farm* and you paid me back by stitching me up in your article.'

Her face fell. 'Oh. You remember that?'

'Yes I do,' I said. 'Now would you mind just turning round and pissing off.'

'What?'

'Print that if you want,' I said. 'I was nice to you last time and that was a mistake. Now I'm being nasty. Piss off.'

The cast roared their approval behind me. 'Yeah. Well done, Frazer!'

I toasted her with my glass and turned my back on her. Revenge, for once, was sweet.

That was the last I saw of the press, except for one more episode. Two mornings later there was a familiar tap at the cottage door. *I don't believe it!* I looked round and there was a man with an open cheque book pressed to the window, mouthing, 'My editor says, "Name your price".'

'No.'

'He'll go to £25,000.'

Now, £25,000 was a lot of money back then and I wasn't making that much at Pilochry. But I couldn't do it so I sent him away.

The following morning, there he was again. He said, 'Open the door.'

'I told you,' I shouted through the window. 'I'm not interested in the money!'

'No, trust me,' he answered. 'This isn't about articles. Open the door.'

With a heavy heart I opened the conservatory door. 'OK. What?'

He put his hand out. I looked at it. There was no money in it. No cheque book.

'Put it there,' he said. 'I'd like to shake your hand.'

'Why?'

'Because I went back to my editor and told him that every man has his price, I think twenty-five grand will buy the story. And you turned it down. You've proved me wrong. Not everybody has their price.'

He shook my hand, got into his car and drove off. And I never saw another reporter or photographer in Pitlochry again.

David Dein, my great friend and vice-chairman of Arsenal FC, rang me out of the blue and said, 'Come on down.' I had a matinee of *Hedda* to do and then a couple of days off and so after the show I drove down to his place for a wonderful evening. I must admit I sank quite a few glasses of wine that night; to be honest I was drowning my sorrows.

Dave had a beautiful, warm outdoor swimming pool and I was sitting in the water looking up at this gorgeous, clear, starry night. *How romantic,* I thought. *And how completely wasted on me, sitting here on my own.*

Barbara, his wife (who incidentally happens to be a dead-ringer for Stephanie Powers), came over and said, 'We're off to bed.'

'Don't worry about me. I'll be up in a while,' I told her.

About three o'clock in the morning I was lying in bed and my shoulders were cold. I went to pull the covers over me, but they wouldn't pull up. In fact they were dripping wet. I opened my eyes and looked down and I was still in the swimming pool. I had fallen asleep in the warm water with my head on one of the steps. Boy! I woke with a start. I could have drowned …

And then that thought went through my head: *Frazer, maybe you should just slip away into the water. It might be the best thing for everyone.*

I was thinking the unthinkable. But I did contemplate it that night. Sometimes I scare even myself.

My agent tracked me down at David's and phoned me the next day with an offer to play myself in an episode of the comedy series *Duty Free* for Yorkshire Television. I was to play myself as a celebrity womaniser shooting a commercial in Spain and chasing all the girls. Which was so unlike me!

I was a bit unsure about playing myself, but that afternoon on TV I happened to see an old rerun of an episode of Lucille Ball's *The Lucy Show* in which Richard Burton played himself. He was trying to smuggle himself out of a theatre and he put these overalls on which had 'Acme Boiler Company' printed on them. Lucille Ball was waiting to get his autograph.

He sneaked out the back door and she went, 'Aha! Got you!'

Burton thought the game was up.

'I've been waiting for you all day. Come back to my house,' she said.

'I can't come home with you.'

'You work for the Acme Boiler Company.'

'Yes …' answered Burton.

'I've been waiting all day for you to come and fix my boiler.'

So Richard Burton sent himself up, and even Liz Taylor joined in the fun at the end.

When the show finished, I rang my agent.

'If Richard Burton can send himself up, so can I. Tell them I'll do it.'

I flew down to London to rehearse the show, then it was back to Scotland to play cricket for the Lord's Taverners, where Nicholas Parsons came up to me and put his arms round me and said, 'Frazer, I've read all about it in the papers. Chin up, old boy. We all love you.'

I felt ten feet tall. Thanks Nicholas. But nothing could prepare me for the great shock that was waiting for me.

I shall spare you the name of one person involved, except to acknowledge that he is a high-profile show-business personality.

I had been tipped off that Gemma was seeing someone else behind my back. I didn't want to believe it but the rumours got more and more unpleasant. I went home one day on an unexpected day off. The downstairs door was open so I went up to our flat. When I went into the bedroom, the two of them were there *in flagrante delicto*.

In films when this happens, the strumpet wife or cheating girlfriend always says, 'It's not what you think!' It's a cliché, but it seems to have an endless shelf-life. As though on cue, Gemma said, 'Frazer, it's not what you think!'

Of course not. He's a test pilot from Dunlopillow. He's a duvet rustler. He ran in naked from the street with a sign round his neck saying, 'Cover me up with your body or I will freeze to death and it will be your fault!' There were a hundred possible reasons for any woman to be in bed with another man.

I considered my options. Shoot them? I didn't have a gun. Stab them to death? I didn't have a knife. All I had with me was an eraser. If I could only rub them out …

'So the rumours were true,' I said finally.

'It's not what you think. This hasn't been going on long.'

I pointed at the man. 'I suggest you get dressed. And *you* … come into the kitchen.'

Gemma followed me into the kitchen. We always kept a bottle of Champagne in the fridge for the high times and the low times. This was one of the lowest. I opened the bottle and poured out three glasses. I gave one to her and took one to the lounge where the man was now dressed and looking rather sheepish.

'Some you win, some you lose,' I said. 'You can have her.'

I downed my Champagne and walked out. On the stairs I bumped into my downstairs neighbour.

'Frazer, you'll need this,' he said handing me a key.

'What's it for?'

'It's for the downstairs door. She's had the locks changed.'

Already! I just looked at the key in his hand. 'Take it,' said the neighbour.

'I don't think so,' I said and walked away.

If the front door hadn't been open that day. I would never have caught them. I haven't seen the man in question since, but if I ever do happen to run into that guy again … it's his turn to buy Champagne, and I hope he will.

I returned to Pitlochry distraught but now convinced my marriage was over. Two more *Razzles*, one *Hedda* and it was back to Yorkshire Television in Leeds to record *Duty Free*. The series had a brilliant cast: Keith Barron, Neil Stacy, Gwen Taylor and the gorgeous Joanna Van Gyseghem. I owe them thanks as well for keeping me laughing and joking when they must have all realised that deep down I was hurting like hell.

I received a phone call from Nikki Caine. 'Dad's having a party at Langan's. Do you want to come?'

You bet! Langan's was a famed eatery in Piccadilly, London. All the smart people went there.

There were always a few autograph hunters outside Langan's, so I signed for them. I looked up, and there was Michael looking at me.

'I wondered who it was signing autographs,' he said. 'Come in and have a drink. How are you, Fraz?'

'Not too bad, Michael.'

'You're not having much luck with women at the moment, are you?'

'I'm certainly not.'

'Well come with me and forget all about it for a bit.' He always is a wonderful host, Michael Caine, and I love him for it.

I danced with Nikki most of the night and I danced with Shakira, Michael's beautiful wife. She actually said to me, 'You know Frazer, you should have married Nikki.'

'The trouble is, Shakira, if I'd married Nikki, you'd have been my mother-in-law, or stepmother-in-law anyway, and that would've spoiled all my mother-in-law gags.'

At one point I was standing having a drink on my own when the great Scottish comedian Billy Connolly came up to me.

''Scuse me, you're Frazer Hines, aren't you?'

'Yes ...' I had never worked with Billy and in fact we had never met before.

'You used to be my hero. Aye, in *Doctor Who*. I always wanted to watch you in *Doctor Who*.'

'Well thank you very much.'

I rose six-feet in the air. When one of your peers admires your work, you preen, but when it was Billy Connolly you feel like a god.

We talked about my *Doctor Who* days and then Pamela Stephenson, his wife, came up and without the usual niceties of saying, 'Excuse me,' or introducing herself, she pointed at me as though I were a piece of furniture.

'Billy,' she said. 'Who he?'

Billy looked at her outraged. '"Who he?" I'll tell you who effing he is. He is my effing hero in *Doctor Who*, that's who he effing is. Don't ask me "who he". I'll tell you "who he". That's Jamie from *Doctor Who*.'

'Oh,' she said. And that shut her up. I never spoke to her again.

I drove back to Leeds and spoke to Gemma on the phone. She was actually quite accommodating. I told her I was due to go away again.

'When you come back, ring me again. We must talk further,' she said.

My shows in Scotland were coming to an end. I watched Excavator Lady come second at Hamilton. I saw a lot of friends and I slowly began to come back to life. I even managed to enjoy a ceilidh we organised to celebrate the end of the run of *On the Razzle* and *Hedda Gabler*.

'Webbo,' I said to John Webb at that final party. 'I really appreciate the way the whole cast rallied round when the press were hounding me. That was really nice.'

'Well, Frazer,' he said. 'When you first arrived in your gold Mercedes for that first rehearsal, we all thought, oh yes: big soap star coming up to provincial us, going to tell us all how it's done. But you joined in. You arrived early every day. You did warm-up-classes with us, you did the exercises. You were one of us. If you'd been a shit, we'd have told the press where you were. But you were one of the team.'

Two days later I spoke to Stanley Sher who was producing a pantomime in Halifax with Duggie Brown. Duggie Brown! One of my favourite comedians. He asked would I like to be in it. I said yes. And that night Excavator Lady won at Hamilton. At last I thought. My fortunes are up.

I couldn't wait for Monday to come when I was to start rehearsing a new *Doctor Who* adventure, 'The Two Doctors', with my dear friend, Patrick Troughton. You see, about two years before, John Nathan-Turner was producing another *Doctor Who* story called 'The Five Doctors', which was celebrating twenty years of the show being on the air, and he had rung me then with a request. Would I be in the story? Well *Emmerdale Farm* obviously wouldn't release me so I had to decline.

But John was dogged. 'If you get just one day off,' he said, 'ring me and I'll fit you in.'

Well a day came up, so I rang JNT, as he was known to everyone he worked with. 'Right, I'll see you next Wednesday at TV Centre in London.'

I caught the train down and recorded a two line scene with Patrick and Wendy Padbury. I was about to dash back to Leeds when John came up to me and said, 'D'you know Frazer, when you met Pat and Wendy today you all leapt into one another's arms and were so pleased to see each other. The fourteen years that have passed since you were last in *Doctor Who* seemed like fourteen minutes. It's as if I've opened a props cupboard, dusted you all down and wound you all up. Would you do some more?'

'Would I? – Just ask!'

Doing a couple of lines for JNT in 1983 earned me the privilege the following year to once again work with Patrick on 'The Two Doctors'.

We did a read-through. I put a gag in, the way I used to. Colin Baker, who was playing the Doctor at the time, stopped the read-through.

'Frazer, love. I'm the Doctor now, not Patrick. *I* do the gags. OK?'

Oh. This is going to be difficult, I thought.

We rehearsed for a couple of days and then flew off to Seville in Spain for the location work. We were originally going to have travelled to New Orleans. I was over the moon about that because I'd never been there. But at the last minute something happened with the American money and we ended up in Seville, which is a beautiful city.

In the end I got on really well with Colin Baker. So much so that after three days filming he was saying, ''Scuse me. I'm the Doctor, Frazer and I do the gags. OK?'

And by the end of the week, it was, 'Look. I'm the Doctor and I say Frazer does the gags. OK?'

One very hot day Patrick and the wonderful John Stratton had been turned into Androgums by the make-up department – weird alien creatures with spots and orange hair. Colin, Nicola Bryant (who was playing his companion, Peri), and I had to chase them. We did a take. Patrick forgot his lines, so it was back to square one. We went for another take. Chase, chase, chase in the heat past the camera. Patrick got something else wrong. He spoiled four takes. After the fifth take, Peter Moffatt, the director, said, 'Cut! All right, let's go again.'

'Why, for God's sake, do we have to do it again in all this heat?' Colin asked.

'Because, Colin,' Peter said, 'you've still got your sunglasses on.'

I was in a good mood and so rang Gemma that night.

'What do you want?' said the frosty voice on the other end of the phone.

'You told me to ring you from Seville.'

'I did?'

'Yes, because we're going to have dinner when I get back.'

'I don't think so.' And Gemma put the phone down.

Well, that's it, I thought.

In Seville we had an interpreter called Mercedes. She was as beautiful, sleek and stylish as the car. She called me her 'naughty English boy'. It looks absurd when you write it down, but you should have heard her say it! Mercedes was married but reading between the lines, it wasn't going too well so I took her out a couple of times. It was nice to be in the company of a woman again who smiled at you. I began to think that maybe there was life after Gemma Craven.

The year had taken its toll however, and after I finished *Doctor Who*, I decided that what I needed was a couple of weeks holiday. On my return I got yet another awful phone call. It was Yorkshire Television. Toke Townley, who played Sam Pearson on *Emmerdale Farm*, had died in real life.

I put the phone down and thought, *When will 1984 ever end?* Although I'd left the show I'd said that if any time they thought Joe should be back, then I would oblige. So Joe briefly returned when I filmed the episodes where Joe came back from France and went to his grandad's funeral. Toke was a real eccentric, but a brilliant flute player and he was like a real grandfather to me. He was always offering advice and he'd had my grandfather's sense of humour.

During my time making 'The Two Doctors', Patrick Troughton and Colin Baker had been on to an American called Norman Rubenstein who was producing a Chicago-based *Doctor Who* convention, telling him, 'You've got to have Frazer. He's great fun. Have him at the convention.'

They eventually wore Norman down and I got a phone call and air-tickets and off I flew to Chicago for my first ever *Doctor Who* convention. Chicago was great. The Americans are very hospitable and very good at that sort of thing. They knew that vodka and tonic was my favourite drink, so they made sure there was a vodka and tonic in my hand all the time I was there. They showed me all the sights and I did my first panels: I thoroughly enjoyed myself.

The panels are great fun. Somebody introduces you and you walk out on stage to be greeted by a couple of thousand American fans of the show, cheering, applause, and many flashbulbs. You sit down and it's a question-and-answer session about your role. Or if you are a writer, the episodes you have written, and so on. I suppose I am lucky: I have total recall when it comes to answering their well-rehearsed questions. I can remember the merest detail. It's helped with this book I can tell you!

The thing I didn't enjoy was the poster signing. Norman had organised a pile of about a hundred posters which, he said, 'It was mandatory for you to sign.' So I would sit there signing and a gofer (a fan who has volunteered to help – they 'go for' things for the organisers and guests, hence 'gofer') would take away the signed posters and bring new ones. There would be pizza, poster, pizza, poster. At the end we worked out that crafty old Norman had made us sign about a *thousand* posters!

Back from Chicago I was jet-lagged but fairly happy. I had few days off before starting rehearsals for a pantomime. Excavator Lady ran at Wetherby at the *Emmerdale Farm* Race Day on the Saturday, so of course I went along. Excavator Lady came in third at 33 to 1. And we all had a nice touch (an each-way bet).

Let me explain the *Emmerdale Farm* Race Day. It was the idea of Tony Preston (more of him later) and our then producer Anne Gibbons – a tall Scottish lady who loved her cast and her racing. It's held at Wetherby race course in December and one of the races is named after our show. All cast go along for a 'reet good day aat' and we present a trophy to the winner of the race. Then they are invited back to our marquee for a drink.

I was proudly looking over my mare in the winner's enclosure, when I happened to spot an old friend, Sarah (who, like me, was an amateur jockey but is also a very private person and so I will not mention her surname in this book). I walked over to her and of course she too had been reading the papers.

'I'm sorry your marriage didn't work out,' she said.

'I am too. But you,' I said. 'You must be happily married now. Last time I saw you, you were engaged.'

'No,' she answered. 'My engagement was broken off.'

Ping! went my heart. I looked at her. She was a very attractive lady.

'So, do you fancy dinner tonight? We could cry on each other's shoulders.'

'What a good idea!'

The name 'Gemma Craven' was fading rapidly from my memory. In fact I now called her Marinade. If ever I have to refer to her, that's the name I prefer to use. Why? Because she left me overnight.

Chapter Nine
Taking Stock
(... take one Oxo cube)

I had saved a little money and decided to take a year off. I had no wife or family to support so I figured I was in a position to pursue my other main interest.

I wanted to retire Excavator Lady and start to breed from her. Before that I was determined to ride her in as many amateur races as possible. So I threw myself into a fitness regime.

George Moore, who had trained her ever since she was brought to him as a yearling, was quite sad when I told him that this would be her last season.

'But worse than that,' I told him. 'I want to ride her out as much as possible, so I'm going to move her to Wetherby with Richard and Liz Whitaker. They'll train her and I'll be able to ride her from my little cottage at Boston Spa every morning.' (I had moved there after my split with Marinade.)

George was saddened not to be training Excavator Lady for her last season, but philosophical about it. In fact he was so good about it all that years later when I was looking for a trainer for my horses Glenugie and Hobb's Choice, I went to him.

Excavator Lady was to have one last run in George's care. It was the Worshipful Company of Farriers race at Epsom that Princess Anne was also due to ride in. George told me he had entered the filly but there was one proviso: each jockey or owner had to find a sponsor to the sum £2,000. Bearing in mind that I had taken a year off and the money I had saved up was going to pay for training and living, where was I going to find two grand?

I rang Yorkshire Television and spoke to Tony Preston. Apart from helping to run YTV, Tony was a great racing man.

'Tony, I've got a chance of riding Excavator Lady against Her Royal Highness Princess Anne at Epsom. I've got a chance of riding at

In one of the ever-glamorous locations for *Doctor Who* during filming for 'The Dominators'. (1968)

The Sugden's check their ball. Clive Hornby and I in an *Emmerdale* episode where we had to play football. (1980)

The horse has just seen the script! Me on a 'stunt horse' in Emmerdale
(approx 1995)

'Your eyes were dead …' Putting on a brave face in *On the Razzle*. (1984)

A moody moment from *Hedda Gabler* with Michelle Newell. (1984)

Top: A budding Lester Piggott on a horse called Le Piat D'Or.
Bottom: A group of great jockeys … and me … at Sedgefield (where my horse,
Glenugie, was course specialist).

Clive Hornby, Roly Plant and yours truly, with Chris Chittell between my legs, at a charity cricket match.

A couple of charmers discuss who will get the last five pound note. Nigel Havers and I at the charity premiere for *Stealing Heaven*, the first film produced by Susan George. (1988)

Epsom, Tony!'

'So?'

'Well I need a sponsor for £2,000.'

'And you've come to me?'

'Yes, Tony.'

'Right then. Leave it with me.'

Tony put the phone down. Half an hour later he called me back.

'Tony Preston here. Frazer, you're on. Yorkshire TV will sponsor you for the race.'

I whooped with delight. 'Thank you, Tony!'

'Not at all,' he said. 'It's good for all of us.'

He was a great man, Tony Preston. A great man for television and a great man for the racing world. It was a tragedy when he lost his life in a car crash a few years later.

A fortnight before the race I attended the *Night of a Hundred Stars* for television down in London. At the end of the show we were all to be presented to HRH Princess Anne. We were instructed on no account were we to speak to her. We must merely reply to any question she might ask: 'Yes, ma'am' or 'No, ma'am'.

The Princess came down the line nodding and chatting and eventually got to me. I was introduced. 'This is Frazer Hines, ma'am.'

'How do you do,' she said. 'And what are you up to at the moment?'

'Well, ma'am. I hope to be riding against you in a fortnight's time. At Epsom.'

'Oh really?' She was suddenly animated. 'In the Farriers race? I'm looking forward to that. It should be fun.'

'It'll be great fun. We might even have a chat on the way round.'

'A chat?' It was her first flat race. 'Do you actually talk during a race.'

'Oh yes, ma'am. If it's a mile and a half race: you can easily jump off and after about four furlongs you might easily talk to the fellow next to you.'

'Oh, really?'

'The worst race is the five furlong sprint.'

'Why's that, then?' she asked.

'You jump out of the stalls and it's push, push, push all the way ...'

As I was saying 'push' I was miming the pumping motion of a jockey pushing his horse out. It must have looked to distant onlookers as though I was about to assault Her Royal Highness. She, though, was fascinated.

Her official escort glared at me and took Princess Anne by the elbow. 'If you'd like to move on, ma'am ...'

'Just a minute,' she said, shaking him off effortlessly. 'I haven't finished speaking to Mr Hines. Do carry on.'

I told her a little more and finally she said, 'That's most interesting. I shall look forward to seeing you at Epsom.'

The producer was seething. I had broken the rules.

Come the day of the race I had got down to a reasonable riding weight. I stayed the night at Epsom with a retired jockey pal called Mickey Dillon. Mickey had been a stuntman on the film *The Last Valley* and I had also played football with him in the Showbusiness Eleven.

Excavator Lady had quite a low weight and I had been sweating in the sauna. When I got to Mickey's house, his wife, Brenda, grilled me a wonderful steak with crisp lettuce and a glass of wine.

There was great excitement on Epsom Downs on the morning of the race, just like riding in the Derby. National and international title holder Ginny Leng was in the race, along with Maureen Piggot, Lester's daughter, Major Malcolm Wallace, now a luminary of the British Horseracing Board and also the lady champion jockey herself, Elaine Mellor. There were interviews with Channel 4's racing commentator Derek 'Tommo' Thompson and Peter Bromley, BBC Radio's voice of horseracing, and I was as happy as a sandboy because I was being interviewed not as Frazer Hines, actor, but as Frazer Hines, jockey. For me that was what it was all about.

We went to the paddock in the little bus as you do at Epsom, and got mounted. The old dry mouth came back, I was legged up onto Excavator Lady and made my way into the stalls.

And they're off!

I didn't think I rode an especially good race that day. There was a certain amount of jostling and pushing. Most of the riders in the race were used to going round on their own. We trailed and beat one at the end, but even then it was marvellous just to be part of the event and to have breathed in the atmosphere.

At the after-race party later, I managed to have a word with HRH. I asked her if she enjoyed the race. She had, 'You were right about talking to the other jockeys – I had to say "hoi!" a couple of times; it was quite rough out there. But it was rather agreeable.'

'Well, don't make it your last race,' I said and Elaine Mellor, who had won the race on a horse called No U-Turn, said, 'Oh yes, do ride again.'

'If you don't want press coverage, next time, instead of riding under the name Princess Anne, why don't you ride under the name Mrs Phillips?'

'Why?' she enquired.

'Because that's who you are, aren't you? You're Mrs Phillips. Put that down as the jockey's name and the press won't suss it out.' (At the time she was married to Captain Mark Phillips; she's now married to Vice-Admiral Timothy Laurence.)

'What a good idea. I'll still think about it.'

'Oh do, ma'am,' agreed Elaine.

Now I don't want to take credit, even with Elaine, for HRH riding again, but I like to think that our encouragement perhaps nurtured a seed of desire which had begun to germinate. And I'm glad that she did enjoy herself. She went on to ride a good many flat races with considerable success.

I had told my agent that I didn't want to work until September when Excavator Lady would be off to the paddocks. So I got fixed up with an autumn tour of *Doctor in the House*. I had played it years before with Bill Kenwright and the other 'young stars'. This time I was playing for Paul Elliott of E + B Productions, with whom I have had many enjoyable panto experiences. This production was with an old pal of mine, Robin Asquith, most famous for playing Timmy Lea in the *Confessions...* sex comedies and the lovely actress Vicky Michelle. The cast also included

Lynette McMorrow from *Crossroads* and an actor called David Auker, who was a friend of Robin's and mine from the Corona days.

During the *Doctor in the House* tour I had a call from LWT asking me to appear on Sheila Mercier's *This Is Your Life*. Naturally I jumped at the chance because I love Sheila very much. It really feels as though I had a second mother in her and her husband, Peter, was a great friend. I filmed my piece for her programme and then I had to avoid her until it went out. I was terrified that I would let something slip about the programme. After it had gone out I rang her to see how she had reacted. Like most recipients of the Big Red Book she was flabbergasted.

'Darling, what are you doing driving about the countryside?' she said. 'Why don't you come back to your other family?'

'Well I'm having a great time. I'm enjoying the tour and I'm enjoying playing comedy.'

'Well, as long as you're happy, darling. But we all miss you.'

But then something happened that made me change my mind and decide that I wanted to be back in *Emmerdale Farm*.

It was 1986 and I was touring in Edinburgh and I wanted to get back to Wetherby to see my new girlfriend, Sarah (our relationship had begun that fateful day when we'd met again at Wetherby Races), on the Sunday. At the time I had a little red BMW 323. I jumped into it after curtain-down on Saturday to drive back, it was a cold October night and crossing the Scottish borders I encountered some black ice. I slowed right down: BMWs are not noted for being the best in slippery conditions. I changed down to first gear and crawled along at about 4 mph. Driving gingerly round a corner, I suddenly found myself on a fairground ride, one of those where you are spun round in a teacup. I was completely out of control. I spun round and round, managed to get on a straight line and started hurtling towards a tree. I hit the brakes which had no effect. I tried the accelerator and this made no difference either.

I ran into a ditch and came to a halt just inches from this tree. I cut the engine and checked myself over. I was completely uninjured. I got out of the car and found not a mark on it.

It was about two o'clock in the morning, but not far away there was a farmhouse with lights still on. I turned up my collar and put my hands in my pockets and I set off in that direction. I knocked on the door and it opened. I explained that I had a little bit of an accident and asked if I might use their telephone.

'Och, look who it is! It's Mister Emmerdale himself! Come on in, Joe.'

They sat me down and poured me a glass of whiskey. They gave me use of their telephone to call Sarah. The kind farmers insisted that I could hardly drive on that night and they made me up a bed on their settee, pressing another glass of whiskey into my hand. 'It'll warm ye!'

After all that I found it hard to get to sleep. *What am I doing here?*, I thought. *Here in a strange farmhouse at half-past two in the morning.* If I had been back on *Emmerdale Farm*, on Saturday night I'd have been tucked up in bed thinking about where I might take Sarah for Sunday lunch.'

That made my mind up for me. And on Monday morning I called Michael Russell, who was then producing *Emmerdale Farm*.

'Michael, it's Frazer. Is the door still open?'

'Of course it is.'

'Right. I'll finish this tour and then I'm committed to panto. I'll be free around February.'

'We'll write you back in for then,' he said.

And that's how I went back to *Emmerdale Farm*.

1986 is memorable to me for another reason.

In 1986 I received a phone call telling me that my mother had died.

I was devastated.

My mother had been the engine of the family. It had been very hard to watch her decline, becoming frailer and weaker. I had often visited her at the nursing home. I knew she loved chocolates and whiskey, but they told me these things were very bad for her as she was diabetic. There was a time just before my first marriage when I had put her up in a hotel in London. She didn't have the energy to inject herself with her insulin and she wanted me to do it for her. It was an awful moment for me. I just couldn't stick a needle into my mother.

The nursing home stopped her having chocolate and whiskey but I couldn't agree with them. I would rather she had some comforts in her last few years than have to live another ten years of joyless existence. I brought her chocolates and whiskey whenever I went to see her. And if that's the way it is for me when my turn comes, I hope somebody will do the same for me.

In something of a daze, I arranged the funeral. My oldest brother Iain was on holiday in America, but I learned that he would be back in time for the funeral. The night before I rang Iain and told him that mum's funeral was tomorrow.

'Oh yeah, man. I know. But I've just got back from America and I'm jet-lagged.'

'Iain. Your mother has died.'

'Yeah, but we're in London. I don't think I can drive up to Harrogate, jet-lagged as I am.'

Iain never did turn up to my mother's funeral and it was years before I spoke to him again.

Sheila rang me. She had read in the papers that my mother had gone. She offered to adopt me herself, because she was already something like a mother to me.

After the funeral I took off for a few days holiday with my pal Roger, who had been such a support the day we buried my mother, and who had rescued me from the press hounds when news of my engagement to Marinade had leaked. We drove up to Scotland to a little riding school that I used to visit during 1984 for a solitary ride.

1986 was also the year that I started my own breeding business. Excavator Lady was about to foal and I had to find a home for her and her offspring so I bought a small stud-farm in Thorner just outside Leeds. It has about fifteen boxes and twelve acres. Excavator Lady had a chestnut filly by Corft Hall and I called her Double Strand, which was a reference to the work we were doing on *Emmerdale Farm*. It was a system initiated by the producer Michael Glynn and involved two sets of directors working on different scripts in the same week. This was good for productivity, but as an actor you were at sixes and sevens. You never knew what you were supposed to be doing next.

My love life was ticking over. Having split with Sarah, I had been seeing a very young girl called Tracey Williams for six or seven months. She was the winner of a Miss Nottingham competition that I compered and *she* asked *me* out afterwards. She was only seventeen but she had the most glorious blue eyes and a great sense of humour. We went out with Robin Asquith and his girlfriend, Leone, who Robin used to call 'Bollinger' because she was bubbly and expensive.

'In that case,' said Tracey, 'Frazer ought to call me "Vimto", because I'm cheap and fruity!'

Later, I also dated Helen Ogden, the three-day event rider. She lived literally opposite the old location of *Emmerdale Farm*. Her father, Victor, was inclined to dislike me because he associated me with *Emmerdale Farm* which meant film crews turning up and ruining his peace. But after a few of Hines' corny gags he soon came round. I was very sad when he was later killed in a motor accident.

But fate was turning her beady eye on me once more, and among the guest spots that I took on was a quiz show for Yorkshire Television called *Ask No Questions*. I was one of the guest skippers for six shows and every week I would have a different team sitting beside me. One day I found myself sitting between the gymnast, Suzanne Dando and the champion waterskier, Liz Hobbs.

Little did I know what fate had in store for me.

Chapter Ten
Hobbs' Choice

Ask No Questions was a good quiz show and I don't really understand why it's not still on television to this day. The format was that quizmaster John Junkin would give the answers and the panellists would have to work out what the questions were. Bill Tidy was the skipper of one team, and I was guest skipper of the other team for six shows.

We shot the first three shows and I went off to my dressing-room to change for the fourth. I came back into the studio and there they were – two nicer girls you couldn't wish to meet: Liz and Suzanne. I tried to introduce myself, but I couldn't get a word in edgewise. They were old friends and nattering away nineteen to the dozen. They were planning supper after the show.

Supper after the show! Sounded good to me.

'Can I come?' I piped up.

No, I couldn't. They had a lot of catching up to do and they didn't want me getting in the way. Ah well. You can't win them all.

A week later I got a phone call from Richard Whitaker at Grange Stables. They were shooting an episode of Hobbs' Choice at the stables the next day and he invited me over. Liz Hobbs had a popular YTV show in which she was presented with a series of challenges. One week she would be a parachutist, the next a rock-climber and so on. This week she was learning how to ride a racehorse.

I went to the stables in the morning and ended up being interviewed for the programme by Liz, with a two year old I had in training at the time called Joe Sugden. Liz thought it would be fun to have two Joe Sugdens in shot at the same time.

The next night she was going to Pontefract Races to finish the show. Having ridden a horse up the gallops (the gallops are long patches of grass which the trainers use to work the horses in order to get them fit;

168

they are usually about a mile or a mile and a half in length), the idea was to see how that horse and the others she had seen did at the races.

I happened to be at Pontefract and we had a drink after she finished filming. I mentioned that I took part in a celebrity show-jumping event every year at the Northern Horse Show and as she rode she might want to join in. Liz thought this was a very good idea and I promised to call her in the next couple of days with the details.

The next morning I got a letter inviting me to a big dinner-dance on behalf of a spinal injuries charity. This was the same week as the show-jumping event. I called Liz and made a suggestion: let us attend the dance together, stay over in London on Saturday night and drive up to Yorkshire together on Sunday for the celebrity do. What I meant was that I should stay at a hotel and I supposed she would stay at her London house. Liz thought I had other plans.

She cried off from both events.

Two or three times I asked her out and each time she would say yes … and then she'd call at the last minute and cancel. I decided that she wasn't interested.

I was very friendly in 1989 with Sally Knyvette, who was playing my wife Kate Sugden in *Emmerdale*. If you're working closely with someone and you get on together, you do find yourself spending a lot of time with them. You might go out to dinner or the theatre together. You might end up sleeping together. But as my old mum used to say, 'It's not the sleeping that causes the trouble!'

I was doing panto down at Lincoln with Di Davies who played Mrs Bates in *Emmerdale*. It was Di's first ever pantomime, so I invited her to stay with me for free and share my cottage for the run of the show and said I would show her the ropes (no we weren't into bondage).

Suddenly the newspapers got hold of the news that Sally Knyvette was expecting a child. And because she and I spent a lot of time together, the press put two and two together and made five. Once again I was besieged every time I walked into or out of the theatre I was playing in.

'Frazer! Frazer! Are you the father?'

'If it's born with a cricket bat in one hand and a jockey's whip in the other, then you might have a story. Otherwise, no,' I joked.

It was a good thing that Di was staying with me. The press found out where I was and every day they'd knock on the door of the cottage. Di would answer, 'He's not in … he's gone to the gym,' and other suitable excuses, while I was behind the door.

Eventually I said, 'Di, if they come back tomorrow I'll join you at the door and say yes – you've caught us out. Di Davies and I are having an affair and this is our love-nest.'

'Ooh,' Di said. 'You little bugger, you wouldn't, would you?'

'Why not, we'll have some fun.'

But curses! They never turned up again.

After the pantomime I went back on *Farm* duty. Then I got a phone call from an old pal of mine, Geoff Wilson. He used to produce *It's a Knockout* for the BBC and I had guested for him a couple of times. He was doing a new show called *Country Challenge*. The format called for a male and a female presenter and he wanted me. It was to be made in September, which was terrific for me. At the time my agent was having a bit of a barney with Yorkshire Television over our new contracts. My contract for *Emmerdale* ended in June and I sort of expected to be a free agent by the autumn, so I said to Geoff Wilson, 'Fine. I'll take the job.'

The show was going to be made by Yorkshire Television and not surprisingly word got around that I was lined up for it. The producer of *Emmerdale*, Stuart Doughty, wanted to know what I was playing at.

I told him it was true, I was making these programmes. It would take a week in September and we'd make eight programmes.

'You can't do that – you're doing *Emmerdale*.'

'As far as I know I haven't signed any contract.'

'But you will do, won't you?'

'That's what my agent is trying to sort out now.'

When my new contract for *Emmerdale* was agreed it contained the provision that I had a week out in September to do *Country Challenge*.

Geoff Wilson had not been sitting on his hands. He had organised a female presenter for me and he was rather pleased with himself when he called me with the news.

'It's Liz Hobbs.'

'Is it?' I groaned.

'What's the matter?'

'Do us a favour Geoff, don't use Liz Hobbs.'

'Why not?'

'Because she'll let you down. She's let me down so many times in the past. She's agreed to some charity do and then at the last minute she's ducked out of it. She'll do the same to you.'

'I've already signed her up.'

'Great. Let's hope she turns up for the first day of filming.'

After my summer holiday I moved house. I had to do this because I sold the stud. This is not one of my happiest narratives but I'll tell you about it all the same. I had a groom who was living-in at Thorner, looking after the stud and doubling as housekeeper. I began to notice that little things started to go missing. I also noticed that she was running up bills on my account, pretending they were mine. In the end she had to go. The experience dismayed me because the relationship between employer and employee has to be one of trust and I always tried to be easy going. This person took my good nature for weakness. So I sacked her. On the day she left she took with her all my feed bins and food for the horses and she called the local village shop and bought herself £400 worth of groceries on my account.

I tried to run the stud on my own but it wasn't possible. So, I sold it and moved into a house called 'Steppings' on the ring road in Leeds. Actually it was part of a circular move. I was caught in a chain. The man buying my house couldn't complete because the man buying his house couldn't sell 'Steppings'. So I went and had a look at the place and decided that it would do me. One Saturday we all moved round one place like a

Mad Estate Agent's tea-party.

My first phone call in the new house was from Liz.

'How did you get my number?'

'I'm working at YTV. They gave it to me. I hear we're doing a show together.'

'So I gather,' I said somewhat guardedly.

'What's the matter?'

'Well to be honest, Liz, you've let me down in the past. You promise to be somewhere and you're never there. I suppose you *are* going to do this show?'

'Of course I am. Look, let's call a truce. Let's meet up in London next week and make a fresh start.'

'OK.'

Liz had a car-wash business in London and she needed to spend time there, so it was easy to agree a date. I booked tickets for the theatre and a table at Joe Allen's afterwards.

I was actually in the hotel in London when I got the phone call at six o'clock. 'I'm sorry Frazer. I'm stuck in a meeting.'

Of course you are.

'But I'll still be there. I'll pick you up at your hotel at seven.'

Seven o'clock came. She called me. 'I'm still down at the car-wash. I can't get away right now.'

'That's OK, Liz. I'll wait.' I called the theatre and cancelled the tickets.

At half-past eight, Liz called. 'I'm coming through London now.'

'Where?'

'I'm not far from you.'

'So what does that mean, about ten minutes?'

'That's right. I'll see you at about quarter to nine.'

At nine-fifteen, I took off my jacket and trousers and hung them up. I took off my shirt and put my dressing gown on. I turned on the TV and started watching a movie.

At twenty to ten, Liz rang.

'Liz, forget it. You obviously don't want to come out tonight, so forget it.' I said.

'I thought we were having supper.'

'The table is booked for ten o'clock.'

'I'm outside the hotel now. I'm waiting for you.'

'OK,' I said wearily. 'I'll come down.'

I got dressed and went down to meet her. To be honest the first vision of her took me aback. She was wearing a glittery silver jacket with huge shoulders and black knickerbockers. Not the most quintessentially feminine look I had ever seen in my life, *but*, I thought, *I've got to work with this girl, so let's make the best of it.*

But the funny thing is that after a singularly inauspicious start to the evening, Liz and I hit it off and we had a smashing night. As she dropped me back at my hotel I looked at her and said, 'I think we're going to enjoy ourselves on *Country Challenge*.'

'I believe we are,' she agreed.

I made to give her a little kiss but somehow her lips stayed longer on mine than I had intended. And it felt good. We stayed kissing and cuddling in her car for a while outside my hotel. Quite a while. In fact I couldn't tear myself away and we spent most of the night in the car. I noticed that dawn was breaking.

'You had better go now,' I said. 'Or you're going to get clamped.'

She bridled. She obviously thought the word 'clamped' had some smutty overtone in the Yorkshire lexicon.

'If you think you're going to do anything like that, you can forget it!'

'No, Liz. Clamped! By the traffic wardens; for illegal parking. It's getting light.'

The show was a success and we made a second series. After that Yorkshire had to take it off because ITV companies were making cutbacks to save money for the franchise battle. It was disappointing, but at least the show had brought Liz and I together.

We decided to go on holiday together. I suggested a ranch that I had been to before called the Tanque Verde in Tucson, Arizona. We were quite gung-ho for that trip but when we turned up at the TWA desk at the airport we were informed that flights to New York were delayed.

'For how long?' I asked but the check-in desk didn't know. Even so they advised us to check in. So we checked in our bags and sat around waiting. I looked at the notice board. A gulf Air Flight had just taken off for New York and a British Airways Flight was just about to take off as well.

I went to TWA and learned that I had been misled. It was only TWS who were experiencing delays. Had we known that we could have been on one of the other airlines … But we were stuck. And what's more, we were bound to have missed our connecting flight in New York to Arizona.

'I'll get you on a later one,' promised the man at the TWA desk.

Our plane did eventually leave London and we did get to Kennedy Airport where we were privileged to be pushed around by some of the most unhelpful people it has ever been my misfortune to encounter. American airports are bad enough at the best of time; one is always treated as an undesirable alien – 'Don't cross that line! You're not in America yet!'

We were in the holding lounge and worried about making it on to our connecting flight. Liz asked to be released so that she could go and check in for it.

'No,' said a helpful Airport worker.

'Well, OK. But there's a phone there, can we use it to notify the airline we are on our way?'

'No.'

'Here's five dollars. Let me call them.'

'No civilians can use that phone.'

'Well, could you call them for us?'

'No.'

We missed the connecting flight.

As a matter of fact lots of people had missed the connecting flight. So the airline agreed to put us up at a hotel. A hotel several miles from the airport. They took us on a bus past hotel after hotel. *Where is this hotel, Maryland?* We checked in but of course couldn't sleep because we had to be up at six o'clock the following morning for the next flight. We eventually got our heads down around 2am and lay there staring at the ceiling for half the night.

At 6am the minibus came to fetch us. We were impatient to get on but the driver was sitting around joking with the desk clerk. I finally said, 'Couldn't we get on. You know we're supposed to be checking in at seven o'clock for the eight-thirty plane?'

'Seven o'clock? I thought you were on the noon flight. We'd better get going.'

Do I need to tell you? We hit some heavy traffic and slowed to a crawl.

I looked at Liz, 'This is not going to be a holiday!'

At the airport there were long queues everywhere. I went to one of the check in desks. 'Excuse me ...'

'Get in line, sir.'

'I have to check in at seven o'clock ...'

'Get in line, sir.'

'But we're supposed to be on the eight-thirty flight ...'

'Get in line, sir.'

America can put a man on the Moon, but they arrange airport queues with the razor-sharp efficiency of a provincial post office in Wales.

'You've only got one queue here, for all your check-in desks,' I pointed out to the official. 'Even in Majorca they label desks so that you can wait at the right one. At least that way the check-in clerk knows how many people are still due to get on any particular plane. Surely you have some sort of similar system?'

'Get in line, sir.'

Liz and I got in line behind a man who was queuing for a 12.30 flight. A 12.30 flight and we were standing behind him! I went back to the check-in desk.

'You again?'

'Look, I'm standing in line behind a man who is on the 12.30 for Dallas.'

'I'm on the 8.30 for Tucson. Can you not let us through?'

'You have to get in line, sir.'

We reached the head of the queue with bare minutes to go before our plane was due to take off.

'Yeah. Looks like you're going to Tucson after all,' said the clerk. 'But sure as hell your bags ain't.'

It is a good thing that Liz was there to inhibit and restrain me. I don't easily lose my temper but when I do it's not an attractive sight. I was hopping mad. I had to bite my tongue because the Americans are not above throwing you in jail, or even shooting you if there is trouble. There's a contradiction about America: whenever I meet Americans in person, say at a *Doctor Who* convention, they are charming. But as airport officials they could take lessons in good manners from a tin-pot banana republic.

We dashed onto the plane, not knowing if our suitcases were accompanying us. I grabbed the steward: 'Could I have a bottle of champagne – we really do need it. By rights we should be in Tucson, Arizona, riding out on the beautiful prairies of the west. And here we are stuck on a plane in Kennedy Airport.'

'I'm sorry, sir,' said the steward. 'We can only serve champagne to first class passengers.'

'Please. Look, I don't mind paying over the odds. I've brought my new girlfriend on holiday and it has been a nightmare so far. We were really looking forward to our first vacation together and I want something nice to remind us that it was supposed to be fun.'

'We can't do that, sir.'

I told the steward our sob-story. 'Our bags aren't going to be in Tucson when we get there, we'll be stuck for days in the clothes we stand in. We've been lied to, kept waiting and we haven't slept in thirty-six hours. '

He went away and came back a few minutes later with two glasses of champagne.

'Sir,' he said. 'You do seem to have had a rough time. The captain would like you to have this with his compliments.'

Up until then I had begun to think that TWA stood for 'Try Walking Across'. The plane sat in the holding area for half an hour.

'Great,' I said to Liz. 'They could have loaded our bags in this time.'

The captain spoke over the tannoy. 'Ladies and gentlemen, we're sorry for the delay in taking off, but we have two passengers from England with us today setting off on their riding holiday, and we just wanted to make sure that their bags were on the plane. Can't ask them to be cowboys without their Stetsons and their chaps! So please forgive us for holding.'

Liz and I looked at each other and cheered. In that one act of kindness the TWA captain and his crew restored our faith in America. Our ranch holiday finally began.

Liz was a bit apprehensive at first when she heard that we had to be up at seven o'clock every morning. 'But we're on holiday!'

'You'll *want* to be up.'

Well, you wake up at seven and through the chink in the curtains you can see the clear blue Arizona sky. So you leap into your jeans and cowboy boots. You notice that although it's hot, it's a dry heat that doesn't make you sweaty and uncomfortable and you ride up into the hills with the wranglers. At about nine o'clock you stop for breakfast of orange juice and bacon and coffee and a guy gets out his banjo and sings a couple of songs. Then you ride back to the ranch and take a dip in the pool. And you think: *this is what living is all about!* I know I sound like the president of the Arizona Tourist Board, but that is my idea of heaven on Earth.

Some time after we got back from America, Liz was invited to the special 500th edition of *This Is Your Life*, where everybody who had been covered by the show was a guest. Partners were invited, so I went along too as Liz's boyfriend.

There were loads of people I knew at the function and of course loads I didn't know. There were also one or two I used to know. I looked across the room and I caught the eye of somebody I hadn't seen for over a decade. It was Marinade. I expected a chilly stare but instead she raised her glass in a toast. I couldn't believe this, so I said to Liz. 'Excuse me a moment.'

I worked my way through the crowded room until I reached my ex-wife.

'Hello,' I said. 'I want to talk to you.'

'You want to tell me to piss off, is that it?'

She might well have thought that. I was annoyed because every time the subject of our marriage had come up in interviews she had said, 'I knew I shouldn't marry him when I was walking down the aisle, but my parents had spent all that money. I wish I hadn't got married, etc, etc.'

It had got to the point where I had rung my agent and asked him to ring Gemma's agent and say: *Couldn't she give it a rest. It was years ago and it's boring that she is still whinging about him. She has her own life now, she's married again. Couldn't she just tell the press how happy she is now and forget the bad old days?*

So it was, 'Hello, Gemma. I want to talk to you.'

'You want to tell me to piss off?'

'No, I want you to tell me how you make Diaghilevs.'

She was hugely disconcerted. 'What?'

'When we were married I was doing panto with Lance Percival and every time he dropped me off from rehearsals you used to make us a drink called Diaghilevs. And I've never since known how to make them.'

'Well, it's a large vodka with ice and that pink Russian drink with mixer and lemon. And that's it.'

'Fine,' I said and then her current husband came and took her arm and led her away. And that's the only time I've spoken to my ex-wife in all those years. That is until I was starring in a panto in Hull and she was appearing at the Hull Truck Theatre. We met in a pub and I hugged her and gave her a big kiss. I think she was slightly put out as in the past she had always dissed me to the press. By this time I was divorced from Liz and I remarked about how we had chosen badly for our second partners.

Gemma found it difficult to understand why I was being so nice to her, in spite of how she had treated me in the past. In the end she became a bit twitchy and took her leave. I've not seen her since then. But I'd like to say that next time I bump into her, I hope we can put the past behind us and have a drink together like old friends.

Liz and I were not only in love now, but wanted to live together. We decided to rent a little romantic cottage in the hills above Halifax. I rented Steppings out to another couple.

Windy Bank Cottage was a wonderful old cottage and we were happy. So I was a touch disconcerted one morning when Liz announced out of the blue that she was moving out. I couldn't understand why.

'Well, I don't think you want to get married.'

'Of course I do. It just takes me time to work up to it.'

'No, I don't think you do, Frazer. I think you're just saying it.'

And with that she was up and out of my life.

I tried to win her back but nothing I tried had any effect. We stayed in contact by telephone but whenever I brought up the subject of reconciliation, her response was. 'No way.'

During one of our phone calls we had the granddaddy of a row.

'That's it!' said Liz. 'Don't ever call me again!'

I went on location the next morning and had a strange experience. Margaret, our *Emmerdale* coach driver, was a medium: she was psychic. She stopped me as I was getting off the bus.

'Frazer,' she said. 'You're getting married in November.'

'Oh yes, Margaret, to whom? It's May now. Liz and I just split up. I can't really see me meeting somebody between now and November and marrying them.'

'I'm telling you chuck. As you stepped off the bus just now I saw wedding bells above your head and the date sometime in November.'

I visited a friend on my way home that day, a man called John Foster, in Rawdon near Leeds. Funnily enough he, too, had a faculty of seeing into the future.

'Frazer,' he said. 'You have great joy coming up. You and Liz are going to get back together on 14 May.'

'What? You can't be right about this one, John. I mean I know you've been right about things before, but Liz and I just had the most awful row. This time you're off the mark.'

Now when confidence is down and you feel lower than a snake's belly, it's lovely when a beautiful blonde phones you and invites you away for a couple of days. Claire King, who played Kim Tate in *Emmerdale*, rang at the right moment.

In the circumstance I didn't feel like it.

'But,' said Claire. 'We're supposed to be riding in the Comic Relief race at Cheltenham.'

'I don't feel funny,' I said.

'Look. I've booked the hotel and we'll be in time to see the Cheltenham Gold Cup,' she insisted.

Well I went, we backed the winner of the Gold Cup and had supper. She took me under her wing and looked after me and as she sat drying her hair in the morning in her dressing gown, I considered making a pass at her. But I'd already had one big knock back, my confidence couldn't take another. Besides it might have upset her. She was a good friend and that's what friends are for.

I'll never be able to thank enough two people who helped Liz and I sort ourselves out. Derek and Debra Franks had been friends for quite some years. I'd known them when they lived in Bradford, having first been introduced to Derek through Carl Gresham, when they shared an artiste's management office together. Derek managed Gerry and the Pacemakers and several other successes of our generation; at that time Derek also managed Liz.

'Come over to us and stay Fraz,' Derek seemed to realise my state of mind.

I needed people who knew us both and understood and they and their daughters Nicola and Kirsty were wonderful. Derek started playing Cupid.

'I spoke to Liz today and told her I needed to see her in York at the offices and told her it would be nice if she came and saw my horse work up the gallops this week.'

'But Derek,' I protested. 'You asked *me* to come with you to the gallops.

'I know. Aren't I naughty?'

The scene was set. Liz came up to meet Derek, after dropping off her beloved dog Salko at the vets for a little operation. I arranged to meet Derek at a pub on the way to the gallops. When his car pulled into the car park, you should have seen the look on her face! I seized the opportunity and the car door handle, wrenched it open and gave her a welcoming kiss, before she had chance to protest. We had a lovely day: walking, lunch, long talks – the chemistry between us was never stronger.

'Please come home, love. I miss you so much.'

'I must go,' she said. 'I have to pick up Salko.'

And in an instant she was gone again. I got back to Derek's feeling as the day before.

'Oh dear, oh dear. Come on Fraz, cheer up!' said Derek.

'She's gone again,' I moaned.

'She'll be back; the way she looked at you is the look of a woman still in love. Tell her you'll buy the house in York and settle here. It's where she wants to be y'know.'

I didn't have the chance. Four hours later the phone rang. It was Liz, in floods of tears, calling from her car phone. Salko was dead, put down after cancer was diagnosed. Liz was devastated and so was I: we both loved that dog so much. For my part I was touched that the first person Liz needed was me. She buried him in the garden of her parents' home in St Albans and I rang her the next day.

Her parents, Peter and Jackie, were not keen on our getting back together. If we split up, they reasoned, there must have been a good reason why. If Liz had been hurt, they didn't want me to hurt her again. So I didn't want to go through them and they were monitoring her calls.

I rang Liz on her mobile phone on 14 May (remember that was the day that John Foster had said we would get back together) and spoke to her in her bedroom, out of her parents' earshot. I said that I wouldn't be able to speak to her for a couple of weeks because I was going on holiday.

'Where to?'

I was going on a Caribbean cruise.

'Who with?' she asked.

'Nobody. I'm going on my own.'

'Couldn't I come?'

'Nothing would give me greater pleasure than to take you, but will your parents let you go?'

'I'm a big girl now. I can do what I want.'

I called Cunard straight away. I had booked a double cabin because I didn't want to share with anybody. So the question was, could I bring a friend? Cunard said, yes that would be all right and there was room on the plane. So that was sorted.

Her parents weren't entirely thrilled with the idea but they thought the sun, sea and sand would help her over her sadness about Salko.

The cruise was marvellous and we stopped off at St Thomas, an island famous for its jewellery, specifically engagement rings.

'There's a street here,' I told Liz. 'That I'm dying to take you down.'

'Is it the street of engagement rings?'

'No, but they do marvellous leather handbags.'

Liz thumped me, 'You're doing it again.'

We had realised that the reason we had split up was a lack of communication. We both wanted the same thing but were frightened of speaking out in case we were rejected. But this time I got it right, I took her down that street in St Thomas and she chose her engagement ring.

Back home her parents were less than pleased when Liz announced that we were getting married. They suspected that she was overcompensating for the loss of her dog.

As for my family, well, I hadn't heard from my brother Iain since my mother's funeral. Then before the wedding I got a letter out of the blue saying that he had read that I was engaged to Liz. Could we meet up – after all we were brothers. He was going to Blackpool with his wife, Chris, and he wondered if we could join them. I had a couple of days off so we went to Blackpool and had a pleasant time with Iain and Chris. He said he was thrilled that I was getting married and wondered whether he was invited. I said of course he was. I even offered to fix up for him to join in and play with the band, because he's an excellent musician.

Taking our leave of them, I said to Chris, 'I'll see you at the wedding.'

'Yes, I expect so,' she answered. I didn't notice at the time that it amounted to less than determination to be there. In the event they never did show up at the wedding. There was no telegram, no good-luck card and no phone call apologising for not being there. *Yeah! Typical of my big brother*, I thought. *That's the second wedding of mine he's missed.* So once again I decide that, 'That's it with him.'

I was disappointed that Iain couldn't be bothered to get to my wedding, but that didn't spoil it for me. It was a glorious day.

It is traditional on her wedding day for the bride to change her hairstyle and perhaps to disconcert her man because he doesn't recognise her. I dropped a few gentle hints to Liz that I would be rather thrilled if she had her hair in gold ringlets with roses in a band, the way Swedish virgins come to the altar with candles in their hands. On the wedding day I looked around from the altar and there she was looking absolutely stunning, with her long golden hair and her roses. She was exactly what I wanted and she looked wonderful.

After we were married Liz and I were going straight into panto. I was appearing in Southport and Liz was in Doncaster. We had two days together and then went to our respective jobs.

After the panto we found a house we liked in York, with a couple of acres of land. We bought that and started doing it up. Eventually we had a honeymoon in Dubai, before it became the diamond-encrusted

Blackpool it is today. I kept the destination from Liz, as you do with honeymoons, but Emirates Airlines upgraded us to first class because we were newlyweds and Liz's face was a picture when we arrived. People asked me all the time: why Dubai? There is no drinking, no smoking, its hot, its steamy. But I've always wanted to visit that country. We had a wonderful stay there and both fell in love with the place. It's friendly and you feel safe on the streets. And it has now become a major destination for British holiday makers.

Chapter Eleven
Sweet 'n' Twenty

You'll have realised from this book that fillies have featured quite heavily in my life. Not just the two-legged variety either! Excavator Lady was a broodmare with a couple of foals on the ground and I was very fortunate that Liz took to horses like a skier to water! Not long before we got married, imagine my joy when she suggested we buy a horse between us, which would race in her colours. And I would get to ride it in amateur races too! So, we decided to look for one.

One day I found myself at Richard Whitaker's yard, where I'd just ridden out, and I happened to come across the October sales catalogue. Over my breakfast of coffee and dry toast – I was keeping my weight down for the summer – I went over the catalogue with Richard's form book.

When I'm buying a horse, and particularly a horse for me to ride, I'm looking for something that will stay the distance. Most amateur riders' races are a mile, a mile and two furlongs, a mile and a half, something like that. You've also got to find one that hasn't won too much money because it would be over-qualified. And one that is *going* to make too much money will be out of your budget.

I've still got that catalogue. I can see that I had ticked off quite a few horses that day; one of them was a filly called Sweet 'n' Twenty.

Sweet and twenty – that's just how I like my girls! I thought.

The day of the sales came. Richard and Liz Whitaker and Liz and I went down to Newmarket. We got a good night's sleep in a hotel and made an early start looking at the various lots, going to stables, having horses pulled out and, which is sometimes the most important thing, talking to the stable lads and lasses.

'Does he or she pull on the gallops?' I wanted to know.

You generally get sense out of a good stable lad or lass. One thing I did not want was a horse that was going to pull my arms out all the way up the gallops. They're not fun to ride, they usually jig-jog all the way home. An amateur rider, who doesn't ride a lot, wants something that's quiet and won't rear up or play around: a horse that won't drop you.

We made a short list. Leigh Boy *was* a very nice horse. He was being ridden round by Mrs Robert Williams. We asked her about him and she said he was a lovely horse. You could see he was quiet walking round the ring, untroubled by all the people and brouhaha of the auction. One of the horses I'd ticked off was Shh! You Know Who and he went for 19,000 guineas. Whoa! Well out of our league. No wonder we liked him. But so did somebody else! Nineteen thousand guineas! It's nice to know that you've got a good eye for a horse.

Then Leigh Boy came in. This was the horse we were waiting for. The bidding started: two thousand … three … four … Our limit was around six thousand pounds, maybe seven. A guinea is a pound and a shilling so this roughly translates into between five and a half and six and a half thousand guineas.

Five … Seven … Eight … nine … and finally, twenty-two thousand guineas. Leigh Boy. We really do have excellent taste in horses. Excellent … and expensive. I looked round to see who bought Leigh Boy. George Moore, who trained Excavator Lady for me years before and who later trained Glenugie and Hobb's Choice up in Middleham. *George*, I thought, *you swine.* On the other hand, he went for over £23,000, way out of our bracket.

Finally we came to lot 981. Sweet 'n' Twenty. She came in and I thought, *You know what, she looks even better than she did earlier in the day.*

The bidding started. If you've never been to an auction, you won't know how exciting it is. All that concentration focused in one place, and that pent-up desire reining itself in. If you want a horse, a part of you wants to leap up and shout out, 'Ten thousand pounds!' and stop it all. But you have to be patient. You have to start off low, at 500 guineas, 1,000, 1,500 … and so on. It got to 4000 guineas and the bidding started to get sticky.

We looked at Richard, who was bidding for us and caught the

excitement in his body language. She was ours at 4500 guineas.

And then we heard somebody bid 5,000 guineas. Who was that? Somebody else had come in. We nodded to Richard to go on. Five-one … Five-two … there was a new bidder.

We began to think that this horse was going to slip from our grasp like the others. But every time she walked round the ring, whenever she came level with me she seemed to look at me. I almost thought I saw her wink. *'Come on, Frazer. Go another hundred!'*

The bidding reached 6000 guineas and I thought we're not going to get her. Six and a half … six-seven … six-eight. Sweet 'n' Twenty was led around again and as she passed she winked. Six-nine. Round again. Seven thousand. *'Stay with it, Frazer.'* There was an Arab bidding for her. He wanted to take her abroad to breed from. We wanted to ride her, race her, win some races with her, and then put her into our ever-growing stud.

The bidding went to 9,000 guineas. This was a lot more money than we had budgeted. To be honest, it was more than we could afford. I thought, *We've lost her!* At nine-one she was walked round again. She cocked her head at me as she drew level with me. *'Keep faith, Frazer!'* I bit my lip.

'Richard,' I said. 'She's got too expensive for me. We're two or three grand over my budget.'

'I know, Frazer. But it's a damn shame. She's just right for you.'

'Go nine-two. Give it one last shot and that's it. That's the ceiling. OK? Nine-two.'

Richard made the bid. It stayed with us. I tried to see what the Arab was doing but I couldn't make it out. Nine thousand two hundred … the auctioneer's hammer was hovering over the block. Time slowed down and I was aching for that hammer to fall. I was sure that somebody would go nine-three. Come on …

Bang! 'Nine thousand two hundred pounds to Mr Whitaker.' Sweet 'n' Twenty was ours.

We got her home, got her vetted and insured and I couldn't wait to have a sit on her. Richard, though, wisely turned her out for a couple of days to let her have a look at her new surroundings and get used to them.

Then came the day for a saddle to be put on her. She was a good ride. We were told by the stable lass who was leading her round. I wanted to try her out, but again Richard said, 'No, just let Tony, our stable jockey have a sit on her.' And of course he was right to do that. When a horse, even the quietest Dobbin, moves to a new yard, the first day of the new gallops they tend to pull a little. I stood with Richard watching as Sweet 'n' Twenty, pulling Tony's arms out, came thundering past.

Oh no! I thought. *I've got to get fit, I've got to ride this horse. I've got to race her and work her here at Richard's and she's a puller.*

Luckily, I was already fit from riding out. So a couple of days later I had a sit on her. She was a lovely quiet ride but she did take a good pull.

A horse that pulls will get you fit, but she'll also make your arms longer and I had no desire to be able to tie my shoelaces without bending down. I organised an innocent little scam with Richard's son, Simon. When Richard was away working with the horse at other race meetings, we'd get one of the stable lads to ride Sweet 'n' Twenty at canter first, a nice gentle canter with other horses to get her loosened up. Then he'd bring her back to us to ride a bit of work when you can go a little bit faster anyway, and I would jump on. It was a bit cheeky of me, but not a federal crime.

Richard got wind of this and one day he didn't go to the races; he sent Liz, his wife, instead down to Newbury.

'So right,' he said. 'First lot: Frazer. Sweet 'n' Twenty.'

I said, 'Well, normally, Richard …'

'Yes I know what normally, Frazer. But today you ride her at canter as well as the work.'

So I rode her the canter … and she pulled my arms out of my sockets. I was swinging off her like a child's toy. As I passed Richard's grinning face, standing on the gallops, I shouted, 'I'll get you for this, Whitaker.'

But before I could do anything else I had to pull her up. Well I tried, but she wasn't having any of it. The only way I could stop her at the top of the gallops was to pull my right rein hard and to tuck her head over the running rails of the all-weather gallops at the top of the grass gallops. Putting her head over the rails like that slowed her up and slowed her up some more and finally I had her slowing to a stop. If you've never ridden a horse that pulls, let me tell you, when it finally stops you just pray that it doesn't whip around and start again, because as it stops, every nerve and every muscle in your body is trembling. If the horse spooks and goes off you know that you'll never hold her again. I stopped her finally. She hadn't actually run away with me, but she'd come close.

We walked back to Richard and circled round him as he barked instructions. It wasn't so bad this next time. We were riding a good fast piece of work. It's better because you go faster, the horse enjoys itself and then ninety-nine times out of a hundred they'll pull themselves up. This time Sweet 'n' Twenty did.

Afterwards Richard said, 'Right. I've got her in a race for you. It's in May. At Thirsk. Brooke Bond Amateurs.'

'Great,' I said.

'Oh, Frazer … you ride her.' Of course …

The day of the race was 5 May. Off we went to the races. It was a glorious hot, sunny day. I was on top of the world. Lots of my friends from the cast of *Emmerdale Farm* were there too.

I went to the jockeys' room, met my valet, changed into Hobbsie's silks and stood on the practice scales. Yes, I was going to make the weight; no problem, so I passed the saddle out to Richard. The expected banter from the jockeys began: 'Have you made the weight? … How will yours go? … Will you make the running? … You look skinny Hines!' Soon it was 'Jockeys to the parade ring. Come on, let's have you.'

Well, you walk the parade ring full of confidence, swinging your whip, tapping your book, as your trainer gives instructions: *Stay out of trouble, do this, do that, jump out, pull in …*

Sweet 'n' Twenty had had one run before, but this was my first race on her: a mile and a half. Richard gave me my instructions and I listened carefully. It's a fool of a jockey who doesn't listen to his trainer.

Now, whenever I ride a race I'm as happy as a sandboy right up until the moment when the bell goes. Ding! *Jockeys get mounted.* And at that moment I wish I was in the stands with a pair of binoculars and a glass of champagne. What I dread most isn't the race itself; it's the few moments before the race starts – because nobody wants to get run off with on the way to the start. It has happened to every famous jockey you can name – Willie Carson, Lester Piggott, every man-jack of them has been run off with. But, at least in this context, F Hines would rather his name did not feature in that illustrious company. All I need is for some wag to shout out, 'You should stick to farming!'

Richard legged me up. Sweet 'n' Twenty was on her toes. We jinked around and I got my jerks (stirrups) right. The stable lad let me go. I had a right hold of her and we cantered gently down to the start. At Thirsk the stalls are only about three and a half furlongs in front of the stands, so at least you don't have to canter up a mile and a half as you do at some course. I pulled her up at the start and everything was fine. She hadn't run off with me!

We were walking round at the start, having our girths checked, and somebody in the crowd shouted out, 'It's Frazer Hines! Frazer can I have an autograph?'

'How can I?' I laughed. 'I'm stuck up on a horse. I can't take my hands off the reins.'

'Good point,' he said.

Sweet 'n' Twenty walked in beautifully to the stalls, very quiet. 'Last one to come in,' said the starter. I pulled my goggles down. They promptly steamed up. A quick wipe of my thumbs in the Perspex, then … 'Jockeys …' *Clatter.* The noise of the stalls opening is shattering. *Clang.* And they jump out.

I had my little finger in one of her plaits, as dear old Steve Nesbitt had taught me years ago. 'Don't jump out of the stalls, yank him in the mouth,' he used to say. 'Put one little finger round the plait with the elastic band, and the reins slightly loose, allows the horse to stretch out so you're not jabbing it in the mouth. Works every time.' So jump out we did.

The plan was to lay up third or fourth and see what was happening. So I tacked across to the inside rail, looked over, and there was nobody with me. I was a little bit surprised, but it's better to be at the front than the back, and I let her bowl along in front. She was enjoying herself – why yank her back and sour the horse? Down the back straight I could hear the commentary, 'Sweet 'n' Twenty, still in front by two or three lengths …'

Coming into the final bend at Thirsk, most jockeys take a pull and then kick home. I thought I'd kick *into* the bend and keep kicking, as Steve Cauthen has done many a time; that way, while the others are taking it easy, you actually steal a length or two. This I did. And I hugged the rails all the way round. In fact when I jumped off there was a white mark all the way down my boot where I'd been tight on the rails! We came into the straight and Sweet 'n' Twenty was still going well. I could hear nothing behind me and in front of me was the winning post, three and a half furlongs away.

Two and a half furlongs … and suddenly I hear something coming up on the inside. He switches to the outside. It's the favourite and the second favourite. 'Sweet 'n' Twenty still in the lead. Frazer Hines has stolen the march!'

But I could hear the other horses gaining on me. I pulled my whip out and gave her one, but it didn't have any effect. I tried again with the whip, but there was nothing in reserve: she'd given her all. I kept riding her, kicked, pushed, kicked … but the other two horses passed me. I kept pushing her. And when we reached the winning post the favourite and the second favourite had been there before us. We came third at 33 to 1.

Well, you'd think I had won the Derby. I was so pleased. The photograph is hanging up on the wall of my kitchen at home: me being led in by Jasper, the stable lad who led up, and our grins together would stretch from my house in York all the way to Thirsk.

The next race was to be at Catterick, a mile and six furlong race. Liz and I kept our fingers crossed. We were already happy with our horse, but if she placed well a couple more times she could turn out to have been a really good investment. We really would have liked to see her run, but on the day of the race Liz was working and I was filming at Farsley for *Emmerdale Farm*.

Everybody knew that Sweet 'n' Twenty was running that day and we'd all been down to the betting shop and put our money on her. When the time came for the race to be run they were filming a scene that I wasn't in. So I got out my mobile phone and stood in the corridor to call in and hear how it was going. They were going into the stalls. Meanwhile the scene which was being taped went quicker than expected. They recorded it and gave a clear ready for the next scene. Drat! That meant they'd want me for the next scene. I had the commentary on the phone: *They're under starter's order, and they're off!* It's a mile and six.

They were clearing the take in the studio next door; a call boy came to get me. *They've only got a mile to go.* 'Frazer, you're wanted for this scene.'

'Can't you say you can't find me, Steve?'

'You know I can't, Frazer.'

They've only got six furlongs to go. I had to go in and rehearse my scene.

I grabbed Tim Fee, our production manager. 'Tim, take the phone. Sweet 'n' Twenty is running. Listen to it for me, will you?'

I scurried in to the studio. We went through the scene. As we came to the end of it, out of the corner of my eyes I saw Tim come in. He flashed me a thumbs up.

'What's that mean?' I whispered.

'A photograph.'

'Who between?'

'You … and I don't know the other. Sweet 'n' Twenty is in the photo for the first place.'

So at the worst she could be second. We rehearsed the scene and went for a take. It was a very emotional scene; as we finished it the floor manager cried, 'Cut!' and there waiting with a big grin beside the camera was Tim Fee.

'That's it,' called the floor manager. 'Going on to the next scene.'

I could hardly contain myself. 'So, did we win?'

'Yep.' Nine to two.

We all whooped with joy. Sweet 'n' Twenty had won for us, which meant that we had another mare, and a winning mare at that, to go towards our stud at the end of her racing career to breed from.

She ran a couple more times that season. Once at Carlisle when the jockey seemed to lie a little bit too much out of his ground and she had to come really wide and was beaten; she finished second.

Then I was to ride her at Ayr. We drove up there and stayed overnight. We ate and drank, because the weight was fine for me. I didn't languish in a nasty old sauna on the race track. In fact we even played golf – me, Richard and Pete Murphy, a friend of ours – during the morning up in beautiful Scotland. I can tell you that is a much more agreeable way of preparing for a race than fasting and sweating.

When we got to the track, everybody ate again, except me. When I'm riding I can't manage lunch. Even if I am the right weight; the butterflies eat the food before it ever reaches my stomach! So I had a glass of wine with water and went into the weighing room, away from the temptation of wine, beer, champagne, Mars Bars, whatever.

I put on my breeches and my colours, which were Liz's colours actually – white with red diamonds. I walked out. Sweet 'n' Twenty looked terrific in the paddock. *Bing-bong*: 'Jockeys, get mounted.'

As I say, this is the disquieting bit for me. Richard legged me up. The minute my bottom touched the saddle Sweet 'n' Twenty reared up and dumped me. Whump. She had never done that before.

I looked at Richard and he looked at me: we were dumfounded. He legged me up again and she immediately started to turn in circles, very much on her toes. We had never seen her like this before. I tentatively put my feet into the stirrups, as all the other horses started to be led out of the parade ring to hack down to the start. It was time for us to go with them.

Sweet 'n' Twenty would have none of it. She planted. She wouldn't move. They pulled and tugged. They clicked fingers behind her. Waved things at her. She wasn't going anywhere. Colin Platts, another amateur in the race, tried to give me a lead. Sweet 'n' Twenty went four paces … and stopped.

Richard said to the lad leading me, 'Right, let go of Frazer. See if she'll go on her own.'

She wouldn't move. I jiggled her, clicked the whip at the racecourse. Normally you're led out on to the racecourse, but this time I had to walk her myself, just ride her through all the people milling around, with her planting and stopping. And all the time my heart was in my mouth, 'Don't dump me again. Not on this concrete.'

Once I got on to the track I let her have a bit of rein. We hacked down past the stands as you have to do. Rules of racing; you have to canter past the stands. Then I took her round and cantered back to the start and she was fine. Once my bottom was in the air and out of the saddle she was much happier.

As we came level with the stalls, a handler came over to say hello.

'Afternoon, Frazer, how are you?'

I settled back on to the saddle. 'Fine …' and that was as far as I got. Sweet 'n' Twenty reared again and this time took me completely by surprise. My feet were in the stirrups. If I had hung on to the reins I would have pulled her over backwards with me. She dropped me hard. My neck and head hit the ground at right-angles. There was a crunching noise like a handbrake being pulled, then she trotted off. There's a chute at Ayr, at the beginning of the mile and two furlongs starts, and it's like a one-way street, with no entry at the end, so it was a simple matter for one of the lads to catch her.

I got up and shook my head. My neck was badly cricked, and Hugh Barclay, the assistant starter, came over to see how I was.

'Are you all right there, Frazer?'

'Yeh, I'm fine.'

'What's your name?'

'Frazer Hines.'

'How many fingers am I holding up?'

'Five.'

'Who do you ride for?'

'Richard Whitaker. Hugh, you know who I ride for.'

'Aye, I know that. But I want to know if *you* still know that. You might be concussed.'

Well we worked our way through my mother's maiden name, my home phone number and address, half the 'to be or not to be' speech from *Hamlet* and the prime ministers since Harold Wilson in chronological order and I satisfied him that I was OK.

But I didn't fancy mounting Sweet 'n' Twenty outside the stalls. The lads led her in empty and I crawled up the stalls like a rodeo rider about to mount a bucking bronco or a brahma bull. I eased myself on to the saddle and Sweet 'n' Twenty seemed fairly calm. I got hold of the reins and put my feet in the stirrups.

'Jockeys, are you ready?'

The stalls crashed open, and she pinged out.

I was lying handy in third place, but going down the back straight she wasn't striding out with her usual ease. She was feeling something. We came round the straight, and I changed hands, gave her a squeeze, but she didn't respond. I touched her with the whip. Nothing. There was definitely something wrong with her and we finished down the field. Badly disappointed, I trotted back to the paddock for unsaddling, casting a rueful glance at the winner's enclosure. I winked at Liz to let her know I was all right.

Liz and Richard looked as troubled as I felt. They, too, had been expecting to have this meeting in the winner's enclosure. I jumped out of the saddle.

'There's something wrong. Richard.'

'I could tell that the way she ran,' he said. 'I'll have her checked tomorrow.'

'There's something wrong with her withers. Get the back man to look at her withers.'

'Are you all right, Frazer?' asked Liz.

'I'm fine,' I said, as I took the saddle off the horse and went to pass the scales. I showered and changed and met Richard and the two Liz's, still long-faced, outside the weighing room.

Hobbsie said, 'Something happened at the start, didn't it?'

The race had started down the chute and they hadn't seen Sweet 'n' Twenty throw me.

'Yeah. She dropped me again; and my neck is killing me.'

Of course I couldn't tell the doctor that.

We took Sweet 'n' Twenty home and had her worked over. Sure enough, she had pinched withers (a trapped nerve in the back), the highest part of a horse's back between the shoulder blades. Richard decided to turn her out and give her a break. She had part of the summer off. Then, Richard rang us one night in our little cottage at Windy Bank outside Halifax.

'I've found a nice race for her. At Newmarket.'

Newmarket! 'We are aiming high,' I said.

Well, she's fit, and in good shape, and I think she's ready for Newmarket. It's a claimer, but don't worry – nobody will claim Sweet 'n' Twenty.

A claiming race is a race where any horse can be claimed for a certain price. Which is to say that effectively you are undertaking to sell the horse to anybody who wants her at the end of the race. But you set the price before the start. The higher the price you ask, the higher the weight she has to carry. If you mean to keep the horse, you might place a claiming price of say, £20,000 and then you would carry 10 stone. And that lowers your chances of winning. If you are looking to dispose of the horse, you might put a value of £6,000 and it might carry 7 stone. We had a normal weight on Sweet 'n' Twenty, because we had no intention of having her claimed.

Liz and I were both working on the day of the race. Liz was attending to her car wash business in London. I was working on *Emmerdale*. The race was being televised, so naturally I took the opportunity to watch it. Sweet 'n' Twenty ran a cracking race and finished second. I jumped up and down in wild excitement.

I called Liz at the car wash, 'Did you see the race?'

'No, I was busy.'

'She finished second.'

'Oh Boy!'

We couldn't have been happier.

I got in the car and started driving home. The car phone rang. It was Richard.

'Did you see the race?'

'Yes, Richard. Wasn't she great? Terrific!'

'That's the good news.'

'What's the bad news?' I asked apprehension clutching my chest.

'Martin Pipe has claimed the first three.'

'Didn't you claim her back?' (One way of taking insurance against losing your horse is to claim your own runner)

'I didn't think anybody would claim her, Frazer, so I didn't put a claim in.'

My heart sank. All the way driving home the only company I had was the thought that we had lost her. What was Liz going to say? Sweet 'n' Twenty was *her* favourite horse and that was my prospective brood mare gone.

I rang Liz. I thought I was going to burst into tears.

'Richard should have claimed her back,' she said.

'I know. But he didn't think he had to.'

'There's nothing we can do about it, is there, Frazer?' asked Liz.

'It's the rules of racing, Liz. She ran a good race in a good class field, she was claimed.'

Richard rang Martin Pipe the next day. 'She'd be no good for hurdling, Martin. She's got pinched withers, that's why she's had time off.'

'Well,' said Martin, 'I'll have that put right.' He wouldn't budge. Although for some reason the winner which was owned by Lord Caernarfon, was returned to him a week later. I never knew why Martin did that and kept Sweet 'n' Twenty.

It was a very quiet Windy Bank Cottage that night.

Chapter Twelve
The End of an Era

Meanwhile, back at the *Farm*, Madeline Howard, Clive Hornby and I became known as the Three Musketeers. We ate, drank and slept together (this last, by the way, was merely a question of huddling together for warmth on location). Not for us the Winnebago and velvet-covered caravans that you imagine TV stars enjoy – we made do with site huts. If we had time off between scenes Maddy would come into our dressing-room and we would all burrow under a huge pile of anoraks and farmer's coats and nod off.

But the clock was ticking on my patience with *Emmerdale*. All good things come to an end. Of course, I do miss my dear Sheila Mercier and especially her lovely Sunday lunches which I keep promising to go down and enjoy with her again. Call me sentimental, but I still get a lump in my throat when I reflect that Annie will never make her beloved Joe a cup of tea ever again. But to be honest, cracks were beginning to appear in the mien of my persona at work. Having worn out several producers, we were now on our second Scottish producer, Morag Bain. She was an Upper Sixth School Captain of a producer, with smiling eyes and a lovely Scottish chuckle if you made her laugh. But woe betide you if you got across her on a producer's run-through day.

'Oh God! Morag's in a mood,' we said as she stomped into the studio. 'I hope we all know our lines. Quick let's rehearse again.'

I finished panto and went back to work on the *Farm*. There were frustrations along with the regular work, but there was icing on the cake as well. Carl Gresham, for instance.

Carl Gresham arranged a lot of public appearances for the stars of soap operas and he offered me a gig: would I like to go and open a shop somewhere? Sure. It was a good deal, Carl went back to his clients, made the arrangements and agreed the fee.

I turned up at Carl's house in Bradford at 6 o'clock for the occasion. He said, 'Let's go. You can drive. You've got a nicer car than me.'

Carl had done this to me a couple of times before. This time I put my foot down.

'Carl, if you'd got Ronnie Magill for this gig (who plays Amos), he can't drive, can he?'

'No, love.' (Men call each other 'love' in Yorkshire) 'I'd have to take him in my car.'

'Carl,' I said. 'Tonight make out I'm Ronnie.'

I was happy with Liz, but slowly I started to notice things.

I always thought I would know if my wife was ever having an affair – the secret phone calls, the wrong numbers, the hanging up if I walked in on her, the unexplained absences, the general air of guilt and furtiveness that surrounds it. But when it happens, you don't always see it in that light. So Liz was behaving a little bit strangely. She would take a phone call and then tell me it was the wrong number, even though she hadn't announced our number to the caller. You don't always leap immediately to damning conclusion. What I also didn't know was that she was planning my *This Is Your Life*.

I almost spoiled it though. I'm a keen traveller – if ever I have three or four days off, I want to go somewhere. (I've always thought the best job in television is the holiday travel show *Wish You Were Here*. You see a different place every week. You explore it and talk about it, and tell the viewers what to do and what to see. Sounds grand to me.) Now, I had a week off, so I went to a travel agent on my way home and returned laden with brochures and stuff.

'What are you doing?' Liz said.

'In two weeks time we've got a week off. We could go here …' I waved a brochure at her. 'Or here? This looks marvellous …'

I was so full of enthusiasm that I didn't notice how dismayed she looked.

'… we'll have a week's holiday. We've been working hard, and you could do with a break as well, Liz …'

'You know what,' she said. 'I must just pop down to the shops.' And off she fled.

I later learned that what she had done was to jump into her car, scoot round the corner and phone Morag.

'Morag, what are you doing? You've given Frazer a week off.'

'Have I?'

'He's checked. He's not on location that week and he's booking a foreign holiday!'

'He can't. That's his *This Is Your Life*.'

'You know that. And I know that,' said Liz. 'But Frazer doesn't.'

'And we can't tell him!'

'Well exactly.'

'I see what you mean,' said Morag. 'Leave it to me.'

The next morning before I went to rehearsals the production secretary called to tell me that there might be an extra pick-up day during the week I was supposed to have off.

'What pick-up day?'

'We're short on an episode, and you may be required to fill in some extra days.'

Curses! I got to work and there in my pigeon-hole was a revised schedule which noted that on the Friday of that week Frazer Hines was working with Clive Hornby on extra pick-up scenes on location at Esholt. I went home to Liz and said, 'Unfortunately, darling, we can't go on holiday because of this extra pick-up day. That's the bad news.'

'What's the good news?'

'I can go with my good friend, John Warren,' who was at the time Managing Director of Laurent-Perrier, 'to Doncaster Races.' I was invited with Claire King to go to the Laurent-Perrier Champagne Stakes at Doncaster on Friday.

'How can you go?'

'I can go for the lunch and watch the Champagne Stakes and then be back on location for four o'clock.'

So Liz established that I would definitely be back on location by that time. Again, I didn't notice that she was more than usually anxious about my punctuality.

This all went pretty much as planned. I left Doncaster on Friday afternoon sober enough to drive and to act when I got to Esholt, only half wishing that I had been able to stay for the rest of the meeting, and a few more glasses of champagne.

Then, I got stuck in terrible traffic. I phoned Jools, the receptionist with the great sexy voice, at Farsley.

'It's Frazer, Jools. I'm stuck in traffic at the top of Esholt Hill. Some poxy road works. Look, I'm going to try and get round the other way. Can you ring them on location?'

I didn't know that Michael Aspel and his team were all set up outside the Woolpack, ready to interrupt me when I came to film my scene. They heard that I was about to come the wrong way into the village of Esholt. They all had to scarper into the Woolpack and hide.

I dashed out of my car, threw my Joe Sugden clothes on, and quickly ran over the lines with Clive Hornby. Then we were driven up to the Woolpack. We rehearsed the scene a couple of times. Jack and Joe were having a pint, sitting outside at the table and talking. And then we were ready for a take.

The first take was brilliant. But the director wanted to do another one. We embarked on the second take. Halfway through it, Cy Chadwick, an actor playing Nick Bates, came out of the pul and said, 'Hello there.'

Well, one is in character, and one knows the camera is rolling. So one goes on with the scene. But a part of my back brain was acutely aware that he wasn't in the first take. Madeleine then came out if the pub, followed by more members if the cast. Suddenly we were surrounded. Finally, Michael Aspel emerged from the pub clutching the familiar red book in his arm.

'Frazer Hines,' he said. 'This is your life.'

My first thought was: *This is the best joke the cast have ever played on me. They've tricked the trickster. After all the practical jokes I've played on them! Michael Aspel must have been in town doing Dickie Bird, or something like that, and they've mocked up a* This Is Your Life *to take me in.* So I didn't believe him. He showed me the big red book with my name on the front, and it slowly dawned on me that it wasn't a joke. It was for real.

I had appeared on so many other people's *This Is Your Life*, but it didn't occur to me they'd do me. They'd even done Stan Richards who played Seth. If I thought about it all, I supposed they'd do Ronnie Magill (Amos) next, or one of the other old-timers.

I'd often wondered what happened to the victim once they'd been caught – now I was to find out! I was whisked away, back to the studio with Morag and locked in a dressing room with some sandwiches. I was already wearing a suit from the race, but a clean one, plus shirt, was in my dressing room, with a note in the pocket from Liz, who'd obviously sent the clothes in: 'Forgive me, darling and have a wonderful evening, you deserve it, love wifey.' I was so excited. I wondered who would be there. Did I have any skeletons in my cupboard? Of course I did, Charlie the skeleton who toured with me in *Doctor in the House* and is now in my study at home. He would be there. Anyone else?

It all came flooding back to me: Liz would be lying in bed next to me, quizzing me: who did I go to school with? Who was my best friend? Would she allow any ex-lovers to be there? I just couldn't wait. The time came and I went on to greet the audience. The show was such fun. A filmed insert from champion jockey, Peter Scudamore, Susie George, Liza, a ventriloquist act with Robin Asquith. Friends, relations and finally my old beloved headmistress Rona Knight – what a day and what a party afterwards. I was greatly honoured to think that a television company might think I was worth all the time and energy and bother to do my life. It ranks as one of the proudest moments of my life. Thanks everyone!

Rumours were flying that there was going to be a plane crash in

Emmerdale. It was leaked to the newspapers. It always amazes me how they get the information, but newspapers and wardrobe departments are always the first to know. The actors are usually the last!

The papers said that four of the cast members were going to be bumped off. They started speculating about who they were going to be. We, in the cast, were also moderately interested to know who was going to die. We all had six or seven months of our contracts left to run. We asked Morag if she could tell us.

'I'm not allowed to,' she said and so the rumour mill ground on unchecked.

Apart from the fact that we all thought it was a tad distasteful to have a plane crashing on the village, we were all grown-ups and we thought we ought to know our fates. We called a meeting with Phil Redmond, who was brought in from *Brookside* to spice up our show. Also at the meeting was Morag and our executive producer, Keith Richardson. I'm afraid that it got quite heated. *Tell us now*, we asked. *Who is going to be killed?*

'We'd rather tell you individually. We'll call you one at a time into the office next week.'

I stood up and said, 'We're not children. I don't want to creep through to the headmaster's study for a possible six of the best, and then run the gauntlet of the production room. I'd rather be told now.'

But they were adamant. They wouldn't tell us.

Eventually those who had an appointment with the Grim Reaper were notified, and the rest of us breathed a sigh of relief. I was against anybody dying in the plane crash. I don't believe any of the *cast* wanted that crash. We had already lost several members of the cast in real life. I recalled the day we turned up for rehearsals and Arthur Pentelow was missing. It was not like him to be late. Tim Fee came over and gave us the bad news that Arthur had been found dead in his car in a lay-by. Dear Arthur Pentelow, who had never, in all the years we knew him, had an unkind word about anybody. If someone had robbed him or run off with his wife, Arthur would have said, 'Well he must have had a good reason.'

My feeling was, if it ain't broke, why fix it? Why kill people off who wanted to stay in the programme. They were popular characters who had been built up over the years. But whatever I thought, they were due to die.

The plane crash was due to be shot during the winter months, not the friendliest season in Yorkshire. Also it would be done by the double-strand procedure where we, the cast, served them both. It was bad enough filming the plane crash, which was an emotional time for cast and crew; but it also involved a lot of night shoots. Each of the production teams in the double strand was fairly autonomous, living in its own little world and not really paying attention to what goes on outside their own eight episodes. All the actors wanted to give their best, but it did get a touch fraught when actors received their schedules and discovered they were supposed to be in two places at once.

On one occasion I was supposed to be working with director, Ken Horne, on a night shoot from 6pm to 6am, and when I was given my schedule, I realised I was also expected to be on location at half-past seven that morning for the next director, Graham Wetherall. I mentioned this to Tim. He said not to worry – he would get me a hotel room in the area, so I could get some sleep.

'But, look, even if I finish at midnight, which is what the shooting script says, I'm supposed to be on location at six the next morning.'

'Well you can cope with six hours sleep, Frazer.'

'You're assuming that the minute I finish filming at midnight I'm instantly in bed and asleep. But that's not how it happens is it?'

'You'll get *nearly* six hours sleep, Frazer.'

That's never how it happens though is it? When you really need to sleep, that's when you toss and turn. And when you finish work, you need to wind down. But I had a more concrete argument than that. 'Tim, even if I could get nearly six hours sleep, when do I learn my lines'

'Oh.' He hadn't thought of that.

A lot of head scratching went on, and they came up eventually with a revised schedule which allowed me to finish a bit earlier.

It was very tense filming the plane crash, and in particular for me because poor Sheila was lying (I thought) dead in the back of the car along with her new husband Leonard. You may remember the scene, the car has been hit by the wing of the plane. Leonard was dead in the back and Annie was unconscious, Joe had a long two-page speech to Ma, trying to get her to wake up. Joe's face was smashed up with blood oozing from a big gash on his forehead. It was very harrowing for me to do: you speak to someone and there's no reply. I don't think anyone realised how difficult it was. It took me back to the awful time when I was trying to resuscitate my own father as he lay on our kitchen floor. It is impossible to explain what this was like, but somehow I managed to get through to the end of the scene. I felt hollow but I seemed to get no help from the director whatsoever. At the end of this long take all he said was, 'OK, we'll try a shot from here now.' Now one doesn't want praise all the time, but in this situation, a pat on the back wouldn't have gone amiss. At least I had my Liz to go home to, although I did give her a shock when I omitted to remove the blood from my face and staggered in the house at midnight.

'Christ, what's happened?' she said as I collapsed on the floor. I looked up and smiled at her cradling my head, concern all over her face.

'It's only make-up,' I joked.

'You bastard!' she said with a smile.

The special effects boys did a brilliant job, what with flaming wings and sheep and stunt cars careering into trees and so on. *Emmerdale* was the Cinderella of British soaps at the time. The media looked down on the show, although they've eased off on it lately. But I think a lot of the press had written off the plane crash before the plane was even airborne. If we had been *Coronation Street* or even *Brookside*, the *Emmerdale* plane crash episodes might have got a special BAFTA award.

After the plane crash episodes we lost Morag as a producer, which was a great shame because she was a great person to work with. She was my idea of a producer. You could enjoy a joke with her, but she had the standing to stamp her authority if necessary. If you had a problem, her door was always open and it is still open to me where she now lives in Scotland with her husband, the writer Keith Temple (who has also worked on *Doctor Who*).

Another great shame was that as all the horses were dead because of the crash, Joe could not go on working for Kim Tate. I found that a great pity! I enjoyed working with Claire King. Combining acting and horse riding was fun, but sometimes scary. I remember a hunt scene where we had a few fences to jump. But on the take we jumped an extra one and then broke for lunch. We walked past the fence, it was huge: 6ft tall with a 5ft 5inch spread. We looked at each other and said almost in unison, 'Christ, it's a good job they didn't show us it first!' We felt the viewers dying for Joe and Kim to get together, but the powers that be wouldn't listen, they split us up.

I don't know why it is that after the actual writers, the first people to know what story-lines are coming up are the wardrobe department.

'Frazer! Now love, what do you want to wear for your suicide scene?' one of my dressers said.

'What suicide scene?'

'Where Joe commits suicide.'

'Don't be silly. Joe would never commit suicide.'

'Yes, he does, lovey. He gets a shotgun and tries to blow his brains out.'

To say I was annoyed is to call the North Sea damp. I had played this character for nearly twenty years and I thought I knew how he worked and thought. He was the one person in the world trying to keep his mother alive. Jack was all for pulling the plug and letting Annie go peacefully. As was Sarah and everybody else. Joe was the only one saying, 'We've got to keep Ma alive.' I felt very strongly that there was no way he would kill himself when he thought she needed him like that.

I had a meeting with Phil Redmond over dinner, and told him I was unhappy about Joe's attempted suicide.

'Why?'

'First of all, it would have been nice if one of you had come and had a word with me. I've known Joe twenty years. You might have consulted me. I might have been able to offer some insight into how Joe would react. But honestly, to hear it from the wardrobe department ...'

'You weren't told at all? So, Frazer, how are we going to resolve this?'

I said that I didn't think most of the viewers would accept Joe committing suicide. How about if we just saw Joe looking at the shotgun, and leaving it to the viewers to speculate whether he would use it on himself or not?

Phil thought this was a good idea and agreed we would do it that way.

When the day came to shoot the scene, the director went over it with me. 'Right, Frazer, you load the shotgun, you sit down, and you put it in your mouth.'

This was the original version. This wasn't right for Joe. Even the armourer (the man who supplied the shotgun for the scene) agreed: 'Nay, he wouldn't do that. I mean, after all, he's trying to keep his Ma alive. If he went, who would keep Annie going?'

Exactly. 'Joe wouldn't do it,' I said. He might think about it, but he wouldn't do it. I've discussed this with Phil Redmond and he is agreeable to playing the scene my way.'

'*I* want you to put the shotgun in your mouth,' insisted the director.

'Well I'm sorry, but I've gone over this with Phil who is the writer and producer.'

They phoned base, and Phil was not there. But they did speak to the producer in charge who said, 'If Frazer discussed it with Phil, so be it.' And we did the scene my way. However, for me it was the end, and I told them I wouldn't be renewing my contract; Madeleine Howard and Fionnuala Ellwood followed suit. I will always remember that when I went home to tell Liz that I was not renewing my contract for *Emmerdale*

Farm she was less than enthusiastic.

'Why didn't you discuss it with me?' she demanded.

'Well, you knew I was unhappy and wanted to leave,' I said. 'So I discussed it with my agent.'

'Well. If I'd known that …'

'What? You wouldn't have married me?' I asked jokingly.

But she wouldn't answer. Perhaps this is another case of 'Hines Sight' …?

I've often been quoted as saying that in the last few months of *Emmerdale*, when Joe had a plane fall on him, was nearly blown up, drowned and was shot, Joe may not have enjoyed it, but I certainly did.

Another memorable scene was where Jack, Biff and Joe had to rescue Vic Windsor from a freezing waterfall. This was horrendous in one way, fun in another. We shot the scene in February when the icy waters came tumbling down from the Yorkshire hills and dales into the waterfall. We were all given dry-suits to wear under our clothing, so we all ordered trousers and shirts two sizes too big for us.

Annie Beavers was our floor manager – first assistant to the director – and a very thoughtful one at that. She supplied a small bottle of brandy for us!

We walked into the flooded waterfall, neck high, and it was stunningly cold. It's said that if you're cold, you shouldn't drink liquor because it thins the blood. This may be true, but brandy on that day more than made up for the negative effects by keeping up all our spirits. We got a little bit giggly standing in that freezing pool while the camera was positioned and the lighting man was trying to light the water. We were standing with our hands above our heads because the water was too cold to lower them. The prop man wanted to hand me a saw.

'I can't take it,' I said.

'Why not?'

'That's my sore hand.' Get it?

It may not be Oscar Wilde, but when you're up to your neck in freezing water that's the height of wit.

After freeing Vic Windsor's foot from where it was trapped by a branch underneath the water, we had to carry him out. Now, Alan Lewis, who was playing Vic, is a big lad and he was wearing a big coat. We were pulling and lifting and carrying Alan, and as we got to the river bank he began to slip from our grasp. We all knew the take was going to be ruined and we all started laughing. Our concentration collapsed and we all four fell into the water. And there we were playing like four silly kids. The water was still freezing but by then we were numbed anyway.

'Right,' said Colin, the director. 'Now you're all wet … I've got an underwater camera. I want a close-up of Frazer's face under the water while he's sawing away to get Vic's leg free.'

'You'd better be quick. It's so cold that I won't be able to keep my head under for more than three seconds.'

The director, being Scottish, muttered something about effete English nancies and sent the stuntman to do the hand shot. The stuntman took a deep breath and disappeared. In three seconds the water erupted and he exploded out of the water, screeching, 'My head is splitting.' When water is that cold, that's what it feels like.

I looked at Colin, and he said, 'I don't think we'll bother with the underwater close-up. Thanks anyway, Frazer.'

I also enjoyed the post office siege in the sleepy village of Beckindale. Especially where Joe shoots it out with the baddies, hiding behind his Land Rover like John Wayne behind a wagon. It was playing cowboys and Indians again, really.

The only disquieting moment was the last shoot of the day. It called for Joe to tiptoe up to the back door, hear something, and then scamper back. As he was giving it a large proportion of legs, the post office was blown up behind him. I was happy about all of this until it turned out that they were not planning to substitute me with a stuntman. Graham, the director, wanted to do it all in one take, which meant it had to be me in the shot, and as I hit a particular spot on the path, the back of the post office would be blown up.

'Will this be a big explosion, then?' I asked.

'Pretty big, yes.'

'Can I see one?'

No I couldn't. They had already set it up and it was going to be of such magnitude that we would only have one shot at it. I suddenly had a clear recollection of Patrick Troughton on that last *Doctor Who* adventure, and the explosion which would have killed him if he had been standing where he was supposed to be.

But we only had one go at this, so I took a deep breath and prepared myself for the scene. We rehearsed many times. We established exactly where I would be on the path when the place blew. They gave me earplugs in case the blast deafened me.

Off Joe went. Tiptoe, tiptoe. He heard someone coming. He retraced his steps. I reached the marker. I heard the *karrummpp!!!* behind me and threw myself forward as though Joe had been hit by the blast. I laid there full length on my face while pieces of Perspex, wood and stone, landed around my head. 'Cut!' yelled Graham.

I was dreading the immortal words, 'Ready when you are Mr De Mille', but camera one was happy, camera two was happy … I got up and everybody applauded.

Somewhere in the press office of Yorkshire TV there is a still of me being blown forward with the explosion behind me. It was in the *News of the World* before the episode went out. I've asked for a copy of it countless times, but nobody seems to know where it is. I would love to have it for my collection.

Having survived all that, poor old Joe had one more accident coming up. He was going to be run over by a car and break his leg.

By then I'd received a script for a play I was going to do in Bournemouth, called *Not Now, Darling* with Robin Nedwell and Linda Lusardi. Also in the cast was little Sue Hodge from *'Allo, 'Allo* and my old *Doctor Who* pal, Colin Baker. I was counting the days. I couldn't wait to do some comedy after all that drama.

So on the last day of filming after Joe had been run over, I was lying in the road and the director said, 'Cut! That's you finished, Frazer.' I leapt to my feet, took my cap off and like Mary Tyler Moore during the titles of her TV show, I threw it in the air.

Emmerdale was over.

Some weeks later, lazing by the hotel swimming pool in Bournemouth I received a phone call from Chris Chittell from *Emmerdale*.

'What's the weather like down there?' he wanted to know.

'The sun is shining. It's lovely.'

'What are you doing?'

'Sitting by the pool, mate. Linda Lusardi has just rubbed some suntan oil on my back and brought me a glass of chilled rosé wine. We're about to have lunch brought out to us.'

'I'm up here in the Dales,' said Chris. 'It's bloody freezing up here. Are you missing us?'

'Chris,' I laughed. 'What do you think?'

Chapter Thirteen
The Bowler's Holding
the Batsman's Willey

I am what I call a Great Cricketer. If anybody asks me whether I would like a game of cricket, I say 'Great!'

Every Sunday in summer you will find me driving out to Aberdeen, Swansea, Tunbridge Wells, you name it, spending several hours in the field. I love the game. And I have the privilege of playing for the Lord's Taverners and the Bunburys. There'll be John Snow and John Price in position waiting to catch a misdrive off your ratty end when you're batting, saying 'Keep going, Frazer.' And at the end of the day you've contributed to a Horizon minibus, or you've raised good money for a local charity. There cannot be a more pleasurable way of doing a little bit of good.

I can bowl a bit. I like batting but I'm not exactly Brian Lara. I did once score 54 not out at Gloucester; I don't quite know how, but it may have been the inspiration of Basher Hussain at the other end saying, 'You're the eighth wicket down, Frazer. We can't afford to lose another wicket,' and threatening to make me eat his bat if I lost the game.

I also take my turn on the microphone. At a charity game it helps to keep things fun if there's somebody on the mike doing a few gags or an impression of John Arlot or Ritchie Benaud. Although Rory Bremner is one of our lot and if he's playing on the same day wild horses couldn't induce me to do impressions.

One day at Castle Ashby I was doing my John Arlott impression when Rory came up unexpectedly. I was embarrassed but already at it, so I had no choice but to carry on. Rory sat next to me in the commentary booth and said, 'Do you mind if I join you, Frazer? I'll do some others but I don't do John Arlott.' Did I mind if *he* joined *me*? I was secretly thrilled to be doing impressions with the governor.

There was a game that found the Bunburys playing in a somewhat relaxed manner just outside Lincoln. Now the Bunburys is a fun charity team like the Taverners. It's run by the effervescent (I never saw him when he wasn't effervescent) chap called David English. He's on the phone every week: 'Hello old boy, got a game this Sunday. Got Lineker, Bremner, Peter Scudamore, Gary Mason and we need you for your spin bowling, be there.'

'But David,' you say, 'I'm attending a funeral.'

'Never mind wear your whites under your black suit and turn up when you can. I'll put you down the order.'

He never takes 'no' for an answer!

The team is sponsored by EMP (Estates & Marketing Publications) a North London firm owned by an old Corona school chum Joe Cuby. Joe comes from Gibraltar and in all those old black and white films on TV, the little Arabic, Spanish or Italian boy was usually Joe. He retired from acting at the end of the sixties to become a successful publisher.

It was a fairly chill day and there wasn't much of a crowd. Joe Cuby got peckish, so he stepped over the boundary ropes and bought a hot-dog. Gareth Charles, one of the other Bunburys, thought that looked good, so he went for a hamburger. He and Joe stood on the pitch in fielding positions munching their snacks. David English turned to them; 'Come on lads, this is a game of cricket.'

'Yes, but I'm starving,' said Joe.

'David …' I said.

'What do you want?' asked David, 'the wine list?'

'No. Could I have somebody at first slip, please?' We all laughed.

Cricket is a great leveller and everybody teases everybody else mercilessly. Neil Durden Smith, playing for Taverners in Gibraltar one day, scored twelve in fifteen overs and was then out.

As he came back into the pavilion I said, 'Durders, that was a bit slow.'

'You thought that was slow?' he asked.

'Well, there's a cobweb on your bat.'

Another time I teased Johnny Keeble, who was the drummer for the pop group Spandau Ballet. He always turned up in a pair of ragged jeans and a worn-out T-shirt. A kind lady in Worcester offered to sponsor the Bunburys with some nice shirts.

'Can you get one for John Keeble – rip off the sleeves, hold it up to the light and fire a shotgun through it, because that's how he always turns up,' I said.

And no – he didn't stick his drumsticks where it would hurt.

But nobody takes offence, nobody sulks, nobody takes the game more seriously than it deserves. If you drop the easiest catch in history of the game, nobody minds too much – unless it's off their bowling!

Playing cricket in this context means that you get to play with your heroes. I was in seventh heaven on day when I saw that Geoff Hurst was boarding our plane to go to Portugal with us. (We play one match a year abroad, and it's amazing how everybody's game picks up in the fortnight or so before selection.) Geoff was carrying his golf clubs and he saw that I had mine.

'Hi, Fraze – glad to see you brought your clubs. We'll be able to have a couple of rounds.'

I had a little 'road to Damascus' experience on that trip. I am a gregarious fellow and I like nothing better than a joke and a laugh, but I can sometimes forget that not everybody feels playful at the same time.

When I got my seat allocation on the plane to Portugal, behind me in the queue were John and Jenny Snow. 'Oh John,' I said. 'Looks like you're sitting next to me – great! We'll have a laugh!' I didn't really register that Jenny pulled a sour face. In fact she was rather quiet the whole flight while John and I were carousing with Geoff Hurst and Kenny Lynch.

There was a black tie dinner that evening at the hotel. John and Jenny turned up for it while I was examining the table plan. I couldn't find my name at all. Eventually it was Jenny who found me. With a long-suffering air she pointed: '*Mr and Mrs John Snow and Master Frazer Snow.*' God knows what the hotel was thinking of!

'John,' I said. 'It looks as though you've acquired a son!'

Well we were placed next to each other so we had to share a table. After the meal and the speeches and a little dancing, after we had enjoyed ourselves, Jenny took me aside and said, 'Frazer, do you mind if I am honest with you?'

Of course I didn't mind.

'When I saw that you were sitting next to us on the plane today I was frankly dismayed. In fact I said to John, "Oh God, we've got that awful Frazer Hines sitting beside us!'

'How come, Jenny? We hardly know each other – I think we've only ever met at cricket matches.' I said.

'I know, I know. We've barely exchanged more than three or four words, but I've always thought you were this brash, egotistical boor who's always got to be cracking jokes and be the life and soul of the party.'

'Well as a matter of fact, that is part of my nature. I do always want people to be laughing and enjoying themselves. I get it from my dad – he would always rather make people laugh than cry.'

'Well, yes,' she said. 'I've come to terms with that. I think my first impression was perhaps a bit severe. Now I find that you're all right. You're really a nice person, aren't you?'

John came up. 'Hello, dad.' I said. 'Is it all right if I dance with mum?'

'Course you can, son. But you're not sleeping in the same bed as her. And I'm not reading you a story either.'

Since that incident in Portugal the Snows and I have been the firmest of friends. If I ever see them at cricket matches John will always say, 'It's nice to see our son doing so well, mother!'

This kind of thing has happened to me a couple of times. But it was Jenny Snow who made me understand that my hearty, gag-making approach doesn't always endear me to everybody. Sometimes people need a little longer to get to know you before they get to like you.

Another time I was playing the Bunburys at Tunbridge Wells. On our side, luckily, was Michael Holding. We were fielding, and I was in the slips next to Eric Clapton and Bill Wyman. Colin Cowdrey was facing Mike Holding who was being gentle with him. With one ball to go, Colin strode down the pitch and said, 'Michael do you think you could let me have one of your real scorchers, just so that I could say I've faced Michael Holding at his best.'

'No problem, Colin.'

Michael took a long run up and bowled. Colin never saw the ball. We in the slips never saw it. The ice-cream seller beyond the boundary caught a glimpse of it as it sailed past him for four byes.

'Thank you,' said Colin. 'Just the one. That's all I wanted.'

I went in to bowl and I put Michael Holding on the boundary for a catch. Chris Cowdrey hit straight to Michael, but as Michael was about to catch it, a white streak flew in front of him and caught the ball at crotch height.

'Well done, Peter,' I said as high fives were offered around.

'Well,' he said modestly. 'I had to catch it. It would have ruined my married life!'

At lunch I was at the same table as Michael Holding.

'Michael, I've got to say this,' I said. 'When you were bowling against England, knocking helmets off and breaking fingers and noses, I used to really hate you.'

'Well, Frazer, it's just a bit of a game you know, just a bit of a game. You try to bowl the ball as quick as you can to get the batsman out. It's just a bit of a game.'

'Yes, and then you have a drink with his widow afterwards.'

'That's right you have a drink with his ... no, no, no, you don't drink with no widow. You don't try to kill nobody.'

And his mighty hands clasped me by the shoulders and shook me while he laughed. I was very glad his hands weren't round my throat.

I've had the good fortune to play at the test grounds of Headingly and Trent Bridge. But one day I got a phone call from David English.

'Frazer old son; got a game for you this season. It's at the Oval.'

'We're playing at the Oval?'

'And it's televised. Sky TV are televising the whole game.'

I was, as they say in sporting context, over the moon. I couldn't have been more excited. 'Brilliant! Who are we playing?'

'We're playing Old England.'

'Marvellous. Count me in David. I wouldn't miss it for the world …' Then a thought occurred to me. 'How old?'

'Well there's David Gower, Graham Fowler, Bob Taylor, Sid Lawrence …'

'Hold on, hold on, hold on. Whoa! Dave. We can't bowl against that lot! We'll never get them out.'

'Course we can. I've just had the exact same conversation with Charles Colville …' As you probably know, Charles Colville is cricket correspondent for Sky TV. Colville, who was a great of the English team had said, 'We'll probably score 380 for two, and you Bunburys will be all out for 80. We'll have blank screens from two o'clock onwards.'

David English had said, 'Don't underestimate the Bunburys. We'll make a game of it.' And Colville had agreed to it. I was still sure we were going to be slaughtered. 'It's the Oval. You have got to be there.'

I drove to the Oval that day with Joe Cuby. To see Joe bowl is something in itself. You don't see the ball. It's not that he's fast, but he bowls so high that when the ball comes down it's got ice on it. But give the man his due, he gets wickets. It may be that the reason for this is that the batsman gets bored waiting for the ball to reach him or has gone home, but all's fair in love, war and cricket.

We drew up at some traffic lights and a huge American car grew up beside up with four Rastafarians inside.

'Hey look, man. It's Joe Sugden. Hey, Joe, how's Jack? Why aren't you on the farm today?'

'You watch *Emmerdale*?'

'We never miss *Emmerdale Farm*. We never miss it!'

This struck me as wildly improbable, that a bunch of inner-city Rastafarians would get anything out of a bucolic-soap-opera.

'Why do you like it,' I *had* to ask.

'Here in the Oval, man, we got no grass. We love the grass of *Emmerdale*.'

'I know what sort of grass you guys like,' I said.

Joe elbowed me in the ribs. 'Well done, Frazer. We're dead now.'

I looked across at the Rastas. Four rows of white teeth as the guys threw their heads back and laughed. 'Do you hear that? He says we want to smoke the *Emmerdale* grass, man. That would be so cool!'

'Frazer,' said Joe. 'That was a bit dumb. They could have been so pissed off at us.'

'Just a bit of a game, Joe,' I said, thinking about Michael Holding. 'Just a bit of a game.'

In the dressing room at the Oval I breathed in the atmosphere, thinking about all the England cricket teams that had done this here on this hallowed ground. To be playing at the Oval! To be in television, not as an actor, but as a sportsman. It was a fantasy fulfilled.

We were to field first. The openers were Mr D Gower and Foxy Fowler. They proceeded to knock us all over the field. The batsmen and the bowlers were all wired for sound so that the Sky commentators, Bob Willis and Paul Allot could hear them speak to them.

Soon they were 55 for no wickets and David English threw me the ball. 'Come Frazer, you have a go.'

'But I'm a spin bowler. You've had a go at them and couldn't shift them. Sid Lawrence had a go, Liam Botham's had a go, why me?'

But despite my protests I wasn't really going to turn down a chance of bowling at the Oval.

Most bowlers don't like bowling against a left-hander, and David and Foxy are both left-handers. Gower toyed with me for a few balls and then clipped it through Phil Cool's legs for four runs.

David English said, 'Fancy another over?'

'OK. I'm in my rhythm now.'

I bowled the next ball to David Gower who smashed it over my head into the safe hands of Liam Botham. I shall never forget that day. David Gower – bowled Hines, caught Botham.

'Well done, Beefy!' shouted David English.

'Hang on,' I said. 'You can't call him Beefy; that's his dad.'

'We've got to call him something.'

'How about Spam? Or better yet, Oxo.'

'Why Oxo?'

'Beef extract!' I said.

So Liam's name in the Bunburys is now Oxo.

Bill Wyman came on to bowl and took the only televised hat-trick ever at the Oval, including the wickets of Gary Lineker and Trevor Macdonald. The third wicket was that of Charles Colville himself.

'You talk a good game,' said Sid Lawrence, as he strode to the crease, 'But let's see what you can do in the white-heat of battle!'

Charles Colville was immaculate in his whites as he faced the demon bowling of cigarette-puffing Bill Wyman.

Bill bowled. Charles could have left it but he put willow to leather. The ball was in the air. Rory Bremner was under it. He juggled it. Our hearts were in our mouths. He held it. Colville was out for a duck. As Colville dragged his bat back to the pavilion giving a very authentic impression of that little yellow duck that appears on the TV screen during test matches, Rory said, 'I was going to drop it and let him score a few and then I thought, no bugger it – it's Colville!'

We did lose the match, as Charles Colville had said we would, but not by the huge margin he predicted. I had videoed the game and I couldn't wait to get home and watch it.

Boring Bob Willis and Paul Allot were dour, not to say miserable commentators. They dismissed me after my first over.

'Oh, they've taken four off him there; he won't be bowling any more. That's bad skippering to let Frazer Hines bowl overs.' So I had quiet satisfaction later knowing that they were proved wrong when Liam Botham caught David Gower off my bowling. I did think that Willis and Allot took it all a bit seriously considering that we were actors and musicians, rather than professional cricketers. I wonder how Willis and Allot would manage if we asked them to appear on stage! Dicky Bird once said to me, when I appealed for a plum LBW on somebody's first ball, 'Nay, nay, Frazer, lad. It's his first ball and after all, t'in't a Test Match, is it?'

And anyway, these minor brickbats pale to nothing compared to my receiving a letter which says, 'Dear Frazer, would you play in a charity match for my benefit,' and it's signed 'Lamby'. Alan Lamb! Another of my heroes.

I drove to Northampton. I strode out to the crease waving my bat in the air as I've seen Beefy and other cricketers do, and took my place at the crease. I blocked a couple of balls and was out for a duck on my third. As I walked back, Lamby was coming out to take my place.

'Ag, Fresser, what's the metter? Got a f-ing big 'ole in your bet, or what?'

I walked back to the pavilion and turned round just in time to see Lamby get out for a duck on his first ball. As he followed me back to the pavilion, I said, 'Ag, Lamby, what's the metter? Got a f-ing big 'ole in your bet, or what?'

'You bastard!' he said with a smile. 'You got me there!'

Later in the same season I turned out for another benefit game for Lamby, a six-a-side competition at Althorp House. The various teams were sponsored by commercial organisations. There was a team sponsored by Oakley Sunglasses and the players were all given sunglasses. I was playing with Robert Powell on the Laurent-Perrier Champagne team, and we all received Champagne. We were well pleased. But the day was a bit of a disappointment to the boys on the Tampax team. (Actually we felt sorry for them, so we gave them some of our Champagne.)

I remember I bowled to Merrick Pringle. He smashed me over my head, straight as John Warren of Laurent-Perrier, who took the catch, looked at the ball and let it go as if it was red hot. His hands were! But the catch held, another wicket in the bag.

My father had been very keen on cricket too; he loved to watch it. It's one little sadness that when I turn out for games, he's no longer around. It's not that I want him to watch me play, but I would love to have been able to introduce him to some of his heroes.

I remember playing against Brian Close and his young Somerset team and there was a name on the scoreboard which read, I V A Richards, but you probably know him as Viv Richards. He was a magician even then. This mere boy leant into a ball which came to me at midwicket. I thought, 'I've caught this one,' and then the ball dematerialised like the TARDIS, passed through my fingers and through my stomach, and reappeared behind me to go to the boundary for four runs.

I was speaking to a pal of mine recently, Paul, who is himself a keen cricketer, guessed that in all the games I have played I must have cumulatively got a test side by now. I did some counting up and worked out that he must be right: in all that time I must have dismissed at least eleven test-quality players. Indulge my fantasy, dear reader, and let this be the side demolished by Hines.

Wickets

1	Graham Gooch	c. Neil McFarland (Sports Minister)
2	David Gower	c. Botham (Liam) (I have the photo to prove it)
3	Chris Chowdrey	c. Scudamore (one ball saving two)
4	Chris Broad	c. At Cowpat Corner against Emmerdale XI
5	Paul Downton	c. A. Lamb (the cricketer not a cast member)

6	Farouk Engineer	b. (first Test-player's wicket)
7	Merrick Pringle	c. by a surprised J Warren
8	Martin Moxon	c. going for a pint!
9	Chris Cairns	c. going for a slash! (a batting term)
10	Darren Gough	c. Blakey (Richard, that is – not him from *On The Buses*!)
11	Janet Britten	c. midwicket with two fine legs
12	Omar Hendry	b. by a haggis

It seems almost indecent that I should have been allowed to share a field with players of that calibre, but I wouldn't have missed any of it for anything.

I worked out the other day how long I've been playing cricket. I think the first team I ever played for was the *Black and White Minstrels* eleven. I found a tie yesterday where the design was a banjo crossed with a scimitar, the logo of John Hansen's 'Desert Song Eleven'. And the tie is dated 1967. That's over forty years of playing cricket for nothing but pleasure. If providence smiles on me I plan to play for many, many more.

Epilogue

My life has been full of highs and lows, but the good times have outweighed the bad. Well, perhaps, too, we prefer to remember the good times. You'll have noticed that I spend more time recalling the beginnings of things than their ends.

Since I first wrote this book back in 1996, there have been many more endings and beginnings in my life.

My marriage to Liz Hobbs lasted eleven years, but has now come to a dramatic end during which I saw someone I thought I knew turn into a complete stranger: or were they just pretending all along? The lady who has loved me the longest, Excavator Lady, moved from racing to being a proud mother, and sadly passed away in 2005. However she is still with me in spirit and I have her ashes retained at my home.

I've lost many good friends: theatre impresario Derek Franks, stuntman Roy Alon, actor Ross Davidson, jockey Graham Sexton, *Emmerdale* stalwarts Clive Hornby, Ronald Magill, Stan Richards, Arthur Pentelow, and Toke Townley, racehorse owner Chris Dutors, and many others. It's said that you know you're getting on a bit when you attend more funerals than weddings, and certainly this is sadly an increasing trend over the last couple of years.

As time moves on, so I've made new friends, and renewed many old acquaintances through *Doctor Who* events organised around the world. I've battled with severe health issues and looked the man with a scythe in the eye … and am still here to talk about it.

My heroes are still with me: the incomparable John Wayne, Michael Caine who, despite his wealth and status remains one of the friendliest and most down to earth people you could hope to meet, and the former champion jump jockey Peter Scudamore who could get more out of a horse than most of his contemporaries.

Over the years many people have asked if I was ever going to write again about my life and career, and all I can say is that there are many,

many more stories and jokes, quips and heartache, love and loss to come. I like to think I am a positive and forward thinking person – always looking to the future and holding out hope for love and happiness both for myself and those close to me. So who knows what the future will bring for me, but I hope that I do get the chance to share more of my life with you.

As I said at the end of the original version of this book, I hope that if I ever get to meet you in a pub or wherever, we'll have a drink and a chat. Life is about meeting people, overcoming its ups and downs and still being able to smile.

I'll leave you again with a toast. As John Wayne (and what a career he had – galloping about on horses, very little dialogue, and all under the clear blue Arizona sky) used to say, '*Salud, amore, dinero y hora de parsarlos,*' which, very roughly translated, means 'Health, love, money, and time to spend them.'

Cheers to you all.

Frazer Hines
November 2009